A
REASONABLE
LIFE

A
REASONABLE
LIFE

Toward a Simpler, Secure
More Humane Existence

by
Ferenc Maté

ALBATROSS PUBLISHING HOUSE

Typesetting by Trufont Typographers.
Printed in the United States of America

Special things to Gloria Klatt,
Jeannie Hutchins and Justine Trubey.

Second Edition

ISBN 0-920256-36-8

Albatross Publishing House
1 2 3 4 5 6 7 8 9 0

DISTRIBUTED IN THE UNITED STATES BY
W W NORTON INC/ 500 FIFTH AVE/ NEW YORK 10110 USA

CONTENTS

For dearest Candace,
who for 21 years has patiently listened to
and helped make sense of my tirades.

PREFACE

The society we have so proudly built seems to be falling brick by brick on our poor heads. Our industrial "progress" has in a few short decades brought the natural world around us to its knees; it has laced our waters with toxins, is about to turn the atmosphere into a sauna; it has lacerated our food with herbicides, pesticides, growth hormones and so much murderous stuff like mercury that it's almost safer to suck dry a thermometer than eat the average fish.

Then we have our cities, which are, as Senator Bill Bradley said, "poorer, sicker, less educated and more violent" than they have ever been. When they are not being burned or ravaged by the anger of the hopeless poor, they are under a constant barrage of noxious fumes, deafening noise, and routine daily violence. And while the hospitals are swamped, the slums spreading like a dust storm, roads and bridges crumbling, and the homeless stacked like cordwood on some corners, the worst is that our neglected schools are turning out a generation of video-game-skilled sharp dressers who are desperately short of compassion, love or vision because they grew up without experiencing any.

Our other social institutions are faring no better. The family, once the stable base of our culture, is becoming a nostalgic memory. What passes for religion has of late given us such an embarrassing group of sociopaths that soap opera writers are turning green with envy. Governments, inefficient, unimaginative, and swollen beyond anyone's worst nightmare to where they are draining off almost half of the average income, have become the domain of care-nothing bellicose fools led by retired refrigerator salesmen and paranoid ex-spooks.

While some of us found all this profoundly depressing, we kept our equilibrium by saying, "True, but savor our standard of living, our robust economy." But now that the economy has been flushed down the toilet with the rest, and is on its way to some white sand beach where it will sit between the syringes, tarballs and blank-faced bimbos, perhaps we would be forgiven for humbly asking, 'WHAT THE HELL DO WE DO NOW?!!'

If such philosophical tremors seldom quake your mind, then you are lucky; but they do mine and, believe me, not by choice. I would much prefer to spend my time compiling the top salaries in the majors and dividing them by the number of base hits to calculate how many thousand bucks you get for a pop-fly and how many million for a bunt—but each time I think "pop-fly" I think "ozone," and when I think "homer" I think "homeless," and the like.

The first draft of this book wasn't quite so gloomy; it's just that over the years the whole world has kept edging closer to the bowl. It started five years ago as a book about our ailing environment and how we could cure it by lifting a finger here, tinkering a bit there. But each time I began to write about packaging, recycling or precycling some piece of junk, the nagging question would erupt as to *why* we have so much damned junk in the first place? How much does it all really contribute to our lives? And, most important of all, how much does it really cost us, not just in environmental devastation but in our being Human? For the sake of our possessions how much do we sacrifice of the most precious things of all: our family, friends, our time, even our love and joy?

And little by little it became clear that over the decades, with each step forward in our standard of living, we took a small step away from simple human joys, away from our passionate, and compassionate, selves. And along the way, our "mad, senseless, unthinking commitment to technological change that we call progress," has not only devastated our planet but has devastated Us, the Society of Man. We have drifted apart. And we have somehow changed from the kind-hearted, secure, truly social small-town people we were not long ago into the mind-lessly competitive, anxious, lonely city dwellers we are today.

What seems desperately needed is a fresh direction to get us out of what Lewis Mumford called, "the increasing pathology of our whole mode of life." To do that we will have to put humanity first again—each human's physical needs and, just as important, the needs of the human spirit. We need to put them far ahead of the mythical importance of short-term profits, special interests, institutions, or economic systems whose preservation now dictates how we live. We need to rethink a big part of our lives: careers, jobs, success—Who do they serve? What do they do for us? We need to examine closely all our sacred cows, everything from our TV sets, Barbie dolls, and houses, to our corporations, education system, and our whole system of government. And we must rethink our grotesque, dying cities and resurrect our ancestral foundations of small towns and the family.

And if we change our ways, if we regain our dignity, our security and our simple joys, we won't need to lift a finger to save the planet. It will save itself and become the paradise our forefathers mistakenly took for granted.

If we don't, if we continue on our physically and socially destructive path, we could soon be as vicious and grotesque as the Iks of East Africa who, driven from their natural surroundings, became a dismembered, mistrustful, heartless, broken tribe struggling only to survive. They, as Colin Turnbull writes, "have relinquished all . . . and live on as a people without life, without passion, beyond humanity."

To change the world may seem a formidable task but that just isn't so. The changing of our lives to a more human scale by each of us will lead to a new world for us all. And if not, you can at least rescue your own family and lead a simpler, secure, more reasonable life.

1

THE AMERICAN DREAM
No Vacancy

For decades we North Americans have convinced ourselves that we were the best and had the most. We boasted
to the world about our Western paradise where even a
child of two has his own TV; where nearly every family
owns a half-empty house, two cars and an RV rooted to
the driveway; where if you sing in your underwear you
get six million dollars, or if you whack a ball over a fence
with a stick you get twenty, and if you trade your mind in
for a ten-dollar calculator you can put your name on
hotels, casinos, and an airline. Well, now the world's
convinced . . . And they want in on the game.

You might think me a cynic, but recent events in
Eastern Europe and the old USSR have shown that people
want not just freedom to speak but, just as badly, free-

dom to shop; they all want dishwashers, clothes-dryers, VCRs, and cars—Moscow already outsells affluent Long Island in $120,000 Porsches. This is a tragedy in the making. To achieve the North American dream we have almost single-handedly propelled all living things on this planet—including ourselves—down the road to oblivion. As you probably know by now, with less than ⅟₂₀ of the world's population we manage to create more than ⅕ of its toxins, pollution, and garbage. To get more personal, per capita we produce ten times more poisoned air, chemicals, and solids than the average Chinese, thirteen times more than the average Brazilian, and a whopping sixty times more than the average humble citizen of Niger.

Now you may say, "Pollution smollution; the wind will blow it away." . . . Hardly. If you don't believe complex scientific tests, here is one that's simple: Put your car in the garage, shut the garage door and window, turn on the engine, and relax. Whether the garage air warms up, turns acid, or depletes its ozone is fairly irrelevant. What matters is that your dearest will be filling out the Widow/Widower Benefits Form by morning.

Of course our atmosphere is arguably larger than the garage, but then there are a few million more cars, furnaces, factories, refineries, generators, steel mills and a thousand other wonders belching poison. And just like the garage, the atmosphere is closed. Just as gravity keeps us poor mortals down, so it keeps down the air— although the air is allowed to jump a little higher. And so the Big Garage is slowly filling up. Now in our small garage we could save ourselves by opening the door, but the Big Garage doesn't have one. So our one hope for survival is to turn off the ignition. But *you* know and *I* know that we're not about to do that.

This is catastrophic because if we continue polluting at this pace the planet could turn unlivable within a generation. Thirty years. But that's the good news. The bad news is that we're about as likely to continue at this pace without accelerating as hell freezing over, because the rest of the world wants the freedom to pollute and they want it NOW!

So the Garage could fill up a lot faster than we think. For example. If no one else but the one billion Chinese, who are already gobbling up $3,000 Swiss watches, reached our standard of living then the total amount of pollution in the world would *double*. You can of course argue that technology could by then come up with some solutions for cutting back on pollution, but this argument has three flaws. One, the Chinese just might produce things even *less* efficiently and cleanly than we do. (Look at Poland where they produce practically nothing but still pollute six times more per capita than China.) Two, the above equation considers only one billion Chinese, leaving out the other three billion oppressed shoppers in other developing nations. Three, population explosions could throw my optimism to the wind.

As to what exactly happens to a country once it gets its hands on some money and starts living high off the hog, take the example of Saudi Arabia. In 1960 when oil prices were at their lowest, the average simply-living Saudi— bless his heart—produced 0.18 tons of carbon emissions from fossil fuels per year. That was *one-thirtieth* of the output of his North American cousin. Then they found out that the world was thirsty for their oil, added a few zeroes to their bills, got rich and bought up everything under the sun—notably cars, desalinators and power generators. By 1987 the average Saudi was belching 3.60

tons of carbon a year into the atmosphere. That is a *twenty-fold increase*. In much the same vein South Korea, which has stepped on its industrial accelerator in recent times, has increased its carbon output by 50 percent in just *two years*.

Economists will immediately object that these were one-time exceptions, but that would be shortsighted. Just as the Saudis got rich with the stroke of a pen, it is not unthinkable that the 170 million, 0.38-measly-tons-of-carbon-per-year Brazilians could hold the rainforest, "the lungs of the Earth" at ransom and do the same. And who could blame them? If we are willing to pay for fuel for our cars why should we not pay for the air we breathe? In other words, we had better alter course because we are headed for one hell of a mess.

The world has embraced almost everything we North Americans could think up from lawnmowers and junk food to Hula-Hoops and Nautilus machines. It seems we need to think up a different way of life because mass production/mass consumption is leading us down the deadest of dead ends. Perhaps it is time we tell everyone the truth: that despite all our gadgets, despite all our wealth, and despite our pants, closets, and U-Store-Its bursting at the seams, we are no more happy and a lot more frantic than our Grandpa was when he was young.

I am not advocating a return to some lost time, because those periods led us to where we are today. We need something more imaginative than regression. But I think it worthwhile to examine what we have done, what we have gained, and what we have lost.

2

THE TRUE COST OF A THING

Fancy cutting down all those lovely trees to make pulp
for bloody newspapers and calling it civilization.
                            —Winston Churchill, 1929

For much of our existence as a species, we lived in a true
garden. While we were sometimes cold, sometimes
sweltering in the sun, sometimes hungry, our air was
pure and the soil we tilled was pure, the valleys lush and
endless, the creeks we fished were crystal clear, and the
beaches where we gathered shellfish were as pristine as on
the day of their creation. And our life was full of myste-
ries, like the wondrous moon that climbed the sky every
night, drove men mad, and even raised the seas.

We walked respectfully in the forest then, asked great trees to forgive us for taking a branch for a bow or bark for a basket, and we prayed to the sky for water, prayed to the soil for grain. We knew the names of all the trees, every bush, every plant, the hundred different cloud formations, how animals ran, how they slept, how they held their heads when the winds came, or the rain. We were at home in the world. It is true that we were superstitious, ignorant and fearful, frightened of spirits, beasts, eclipses, the dark, and thunder, but we had a lot of magic, and dances to drive our dreads away.

Things remained much the same until the Industrial Revolution. Sure there was a booby now and then who wanted to have stones piled to the sky, who, as Thoreau suggested, should have been nipped in the bud. But most of us lived fairly simple lives. We lived in villages and hamlets and worked mostly at home, for ourselves. We grew our food or raised and hunted it. Our clothes, of hide or wool or cotton—whatever was handiest—and our tools, were made by craftsmen in the village, the weaver, the smithy, and they were all made well and lasted us a lifetime. When we weren't working, we raised our families, drank with friends, then died in peace and made room for someone else. By and large we lived in harmony with Nature, were as much a part of her as any beast or tree, and what scars we left healed in little time.

Then something changed. It separated us from our land and villages, and changed us from free men, who toiled hard to survive but were at least our own lords and masters. The Industrial Revolution began producing things in vast factories in distant cities and selling them cheaper than a craftsman could. The weaver and the smithy had to close shop. The revolution dazzled us with things to buy, but of course we had no money, so it coaxed us away from our healthy, airy villages, with promises of secure employment and good wages, into cities choked by overcrowding, unemployment, poverty, filth, disease and crime. We began working for someone else. We had *jobs*. We worked interminable hours cramped in inhuman places without sun or air, and although the work was easier on our backs than tilling soil, it left a crushing load upon the soul. And a peaceful, clean farming town became the rubble of Detroit; a quiet fishing cove, Manhattan; and empty stretches of beach and sand, the nightmares of Los Angeles and Miami. And a relatively easygoing, hospitable, gracious group of farmers and craftsmen became the mistrustful, hectic city dwellers of today.

We went out to the country only on special days. And we began to talk about *us* in here, and *Nature* out there. We began to think of Nature as unlike *us*; something crude, unreasonable, barbarous and strange. Something a civilized world would be better off without. Little by little we lost our sense of reason. "Man against Nature" became our battle cry. Nothing could have suited the new industrialists more.

The owners of factories and the financiers were inundated with wealth they had never dreamed of—and certainly could not use—so they searched for places to *invest* it. And so the railroads were built, not so much because we needed them, not so much to improve humanity's lot, but because they would *make unused money grow*.

And make it grow they did, with a vengeance.

In 1830 there were but "a few dozen miles of railway in the world. By 1850 there were over 23,000 miles." But we didn't stop there. We raised great dams, paved valleys, strung a billion miles of wire as if some great demented spider were webbing up the sky. We strip-mined, we clear-cut, we tunnelled, bridged, underpassed, and over-passed; we built jets that got us from here to there in hours, machines that sent pictures faster than we imag-ined them. We were warm when it was cold outside, cool when it was hot. We grew lush lawns in the desert, made snow on a summer's day. We could out-soar birds, out-dive eels, we could dance on the moon. . . . We had Nature where we wanted her—on her knees. Except the Nature that we defeated wasn't half as dangerous as the new Nature we made.

The air we made is hard to breathe so we take shallow breaths and wait for a day in the country to fill our lungs again. The lakes and rivers into which we once jumped happily now look too full of yucky things, so we take a picture, go home and watch the video. On our beaches, those once virgin edges of the world where we could look off into forever, we now tend to look mainly at our feet so we don't step on syringes and sundry hospital offal. Then there is the water in our taps. We used to drink it with zeal but now we prefer it from bottles, hoping that it's safer because it's from far away.

But the phrase "Man against Nature" has remained with us and is still our battle cry as we chemical-bomb a fly, shower poisons down on ants, butcher a forest, or build a dam and flood a valley the size of a small country so we can heat and cool more movie houses, malls, and bars—the places to which we go when we feel empty or alone and have no villagers or superstitions to entertain us anymore.

And how in the name of God could *we* be "*against* Nature"?! We *are* Nature. We are made of the same tissue as every other mammal on this earth, drink the same water, eat the same things, mate the same way—although we waste a lot more time and money on hair, and clothes, and cars. We couldn't live two minutes without air, or a few days without water, or a few weeks without the food we grow in the earth—and air, water, and soil are about as basic Nature as you get.

We are then part of and nurtured by this planet, much as an unborn child is part of and nurtured by its mother. But there is a difference; the child is born, grows, then goes off on his own. We, on the other hand, can never leave the womb. If the mother is sick, we're sick. If the mother dies, we die. And yet every day, nearly every moment of our lives, every time we start the car, buy a burger, buy a trinket, with almost everything we do as modern man, we are poisoning our mother.

Unless we are suffering from a universal death wish, we must be living as we are because, to put it mildly, we're not nearly as intelligent as we think we are. While we may be good with numbers and swell at making gadgets, in assimilated thinking we seem to be in the Dark Ages.

There have been bursts of resonant awakenings lately. We are beginning to understand that the Brazilian rainforest gives us some of our daily breath; that the curly smoke from a harmless-looking smokestack can acidify and kill a whole lake a thousand miles away. (Two hundred lakes in the Adirondack Mountains are devoid of fish; 1,800 lakes in Sweden are practically lifeless.) We are learning that a Styrofoam cup might save us from hot fingers right now but will kill us with skin cancer later by eating away the protective ozone layer eight miles above our heads; that the old oil or rat poison we dump today might turn up in our own coffee cups tomorrow.

But we have difficulty dealing with abstract threats, so we have turned to something more tangible, closer to home, something everyone loves to hate: garbage. Books have been written, clubs formed, recycling programs started, to recoup bottles, cans, newspapers and grass cuttings. Good. Every bit helps. We will save our precious open spaces from turning into poison-leaching landfills and our air from even more smoke-and-toxin-belching incinerators. We will also, by reusing materials, reduce pollution and save energy and resources. So all in all recycling is a fine idea, but as for halting environmental destruction, it's a bit like trying to stop a freight train with a feather. And the greatest danger is that, as we sort our cans, we convince ourselves that we are on our way to curing the ailing planet. Well, we're not. We're putting Band-Aids on the dying.

And so we drift off into contentment, never asking the frightening question: "Why do we *produce* so much garbage in the first place?"—not only what we throw out daily, but all the gizmos, gadgets and gear that still clutter our lives. To put it plainly, we are choking on the garbage not because we don't know where to put it, but because *we produced it all to start with.* This is a most important point, for as a species we will probably not perish from being buried by landfill, but rather from the poisons, fumes and myriad other wastes all that garbage took to *manufacture.* For garbage is not privileged with virgin birth. Plastic bags did not just appear one morning on the shelves, Coke machines did not fill themselves with cans miraculously overnight, and the mine field of ugly plastic toys your child now abhors were not made by Santa out of angel hair and wishes. They were mined, crushed, trucked, smelted, molded, dyed, packaged, advertised, warehoused, transported and shelved. And each step used great quantities of energy and raw materials, hence produced pollution and waste. But we're not finished yet.

Let's look at the child's toy. To find it, you, well-meaning parent, drove down to the mall, which was built to display the toy in tasteful, waterfalled, musical surroundings with lots of pretty lights and humming escalators—all burning up energy, all, indirectly, belching out tons of pollution. Then you bought the toy. With what? With money you earned with the sweat of your brow and the fumes of your factory, or the tons of wasted energy of computers and copiers and throwaway paper products of your office.

So, you see, you would be misleading yourself if you thought you had simply bought your child a little present. You have done much more than that. For along with Kiburka the jumping-serpent-dildoman transformer, you have also, unwittingly, bought him an added gift: a few hundred cubic feet of poisoned air, and chemical poisons that trickled into creeks and groundwater from the inks, dyes, and bleaches used for refining and coloring the toy, the packaging, the signs, the giftwrap, the gas for your car and the saleslady's lipstick. And if you bought him something larger, say a Rustic Plastic Farm, you then might also be giving him a big blob from the oil spill in Alaska or maybe even an oil-choked dead seal.

Such is the way of civilized man; we no longer kill in a bloody hunt for food—we're refined. We work in clean well-lighted places making civilized movements, and kill instead from a great distance with a hired bucket of oil . . . for a toy . . . or for a plastic bag for garbage.

If we are to survive in a world worth living in, if we have enough love for our children not to condemn them

11

to a life in a universal slum with unbreathable air, undrinkable water, and soil either too eroded, too exhausted, or too poisoned to feed them, then we will have to drastically change our habits.

This time we have no one else to blame. Governments have done only what we wanted. We wanted to be safe so they made us enough bombs to blow every man, woman, and child off the face of the earth once a day, from Labor Day until Christmas. Even when they try to do something honorable and simple like putting less carbon into the air to control global warming, the result seems to be guaranteed disaster. From 1983 to 1988 the average annual increase of global carbon emissions was 2.8 percent. World governments meeting in Toronto in June of 1988 called this an outrage and vowed to *cut* world emissions 20 percent in the coming years. That year carbon emissions jumped 3.7 percent, the largest increase in a decade. And, even more frightening, in February of 1990 the *New York Times* reported analysts' predictions that demand for oil might jump as much as 50 percent in five years, while others see a *sixfold* increase in energy demand within five decades. . . . So much for cutting back on emissions of carbon.

And you sure can't blame big business; it's nothing but our slave. It finds out what we like, then drowns us in the stuff. "You like Barbie dolls? Good! Here's a billion of them. You like hamburgers in Styrofoam containers? Here's thirty billion more." And we helpless, smiling sheep follow right along. But we don't "Bah, Bah, Bah." We Buy, Buy, Buy.

We want everything ever made and we want it now, want it cheap and in twenty different colors. And next year we want more, only a bit different. So big business almost kills itself every year to please us. If it means oil spills, poisoned water and chemical disasters . . . well . . . nobody's perfect.

So you want to know who's guilty? . . . You! . . . You bought the bloody toy . . . And so did I.

We bought radios, stereos, cassettes, CDs, then VCRs. We bought Instamatics, Veg-O-Matics, popcorn makers, muffin bakers, machines to mow the lawn, fry a prawn, shear the dog, saw a log, to blow snow, leaves, hair or air; we bought gear to barbecue a chicken, broil it, roast it, deep-fry it or toast it or put it in a Radar Range and blow it to the moon; bought chemicals to calm our fits, dry our pits, clean our mitts, expand our tits . . . *Have we gone and lost our collective bloody minds?!!*

Or are we simply bored? Have our lives become so meaningless and empty that we have to fill every moment with a toy? If that's so, it's sad. Sad that we might turn the universe's only living planet into a monstrous monument to the boredom of us all.

It's up to us. Each of us. And yet the sacrifices we need to make can be no sacrifice at all. We simply need to cut back on our addiction to buying and hoarding. We need to do more with our lives than numbly earn and spend. We need to think. We need to come alive again and live as simply, freely, happily, and passionately as we did when we were children.

There is no doubt that we can make major changes, not in a generation, not in decades, but in weeks. Maybe we should call this a war—that seems to unite us best. But there need be no shots fired, or bodies mangled, just all of us at home, at peace, cleaning house. And we will *all* win a habitable earth, livable cities, and unpoisoned, verdant land. And some sanity. Some calm, some time to know our children. Some pride in being Human.

There is much talk of the world cutting back on the most absurd junk of all. They say it's not easy. They're arguing about a missile here, a warhead there; inspection, deception, verification. Slow old men, slow old ideas. But it's something. They have finally realized that the most absurd junk of all might not be vital for our survival. If the slow old men can finally come this far, then couldn't we? If they can disarm themselves of bombs, can we not disarm ourselves of junk? If we don't, if we continue with this manic pace of destruction of our planet and our lives, we might yet come to a time so horrible, so inhuman, that we may wish we had saved some warheads for ourselves.

So let's start . . . on Sunday.

3

SUNDAY

What the hell ever happened to our Sundays?

I used to wake up when Tommy Flint started yelling at the fat little dog he was trying to train to be Rin Tin Tin. But the fat dog didn't get fat by being stupid. When Tommy jumped over the fence and ordered him to follow, Fat Dog would amicably amble to a post, sniff a bit, then have himself a comfy little pee. That's when Tommy yelled and woke me up. Later his dad Ernie would shuffle over in his worn-toed woolen slippers, bum a cigarette from my Mom, set himself down at the kitchen table, and nibble at what was left of breakfast while discussing with my dad his garden or the world. My mother meanwhile cooked one of her enormous Sunday meals.

The streets were empty.

Chubby Eddy Emanoff would creak by on his old bike and, like some bemused Paul Revere, try to rouse the neighborhood to a ball game at the schoolyard. Not a soul ever showed up before lunch. Eddy knew that but he liked to creak about on his bike anyway, up the street, down the lane, only to end up lying on the grass at the corner trying to talk Billy Evans into trading his Al Kaline card for some weird guy called Turk Lown.

After a huge Hungarian lunch of three-hour-simmered chicken soup, roast meats with paprika and sour-cream sauces, cucumber salads, and enough buttery, fresh baked cakes to feed an army, I was out the door and running for the field with my mother shouting, "Be careful yourself! What happen if you die?"

Then we played ball. We had no teams, no uniforms, no coaches, not even bases, only an old chipped bat and a few gloves that we shared, and the schoolyard wasn't exactly a diamond—just an old soccer field full of weeds and gravel. The weeds and the gravel gave you strange bounces in the gut and the privates but you got used to that; what got you every time was that right field fence only a hundred fifty feet away; and Al Crowder. The bastard hit lefthanded. Squinty little eyes, cigarette dangling from his mouth, and bang . . . a home run. John Hardy would climb the fence and sit there when Crowder came to bat but bloody Crowder never hit right at him so John would end up talking to Mrs. Thompson on the other side, who was out working her vegetable garden, in her hat.

Anyway, we'd pick teams by sticking our feet in a circle and somebody saying "Engine engine number nine going down Chicago line," then we'd yell and fight over who got to play where. Then we'd settle down and play ball until Eddy Emanoff hit one of his hard grounders to the fence and rounded first base chuckling and puffing, but second base was a bit up hill and Eddy never made it because Jerry Allye would jump him and drag him down and beat him with his glove while Eddy died laughing. Some of us would wander off during the game and others would wander in, and some went over to Mrs. Thompson's to have a drink out of her garden hose and eat a radish.

The best part was when John Hardy's sister came to play. She was a bit older, soft and round, and she was trying to grow her nails so she refused to wear a glove. So she held it. Then she'd throw it at a grounder. And to catch pop flies . . . man, we loved pop flies . . . she'd drop the glove and grab the hem of her T-shirt with two hands and lift it up and hold it out like a net. Then the guys around her would fall to their knees . . . praying. When the sun got so low it shone right in our eyes we went home. One day the fog rolled in and we snuck off and left Hardy sitting on the fence.

Sunday was the day I had to mow the lawn. Torture. It wasn't the time it took; we had a tiny house and a tiny lot, but the idea of cutting this green stuff just so it could grow again by next Sunday?! Jeezus. So I pushed and pulled the old handmower while everybody else sat on the fence and talked. Then we'd eat at somebody's house and end up in Dave Dowsett's dusty basement where a great sawdust-burning furnace roared, and we played pool on an ancient table the size of a big suitcase with pitted little clay balls that rolled every way but straight.

When we heard Ed Sullivan upstairs bid everyone goodnight, we would drift away into the dark, into the fog, and wish to heaven we'd get lost so we wouldn't have to go to school again next morning.

Times change.

I was visiting in-laws in Florida this spring, one of those places with palm trees and canals, big houses, lawns—great big bloody lawns—and I tried to sleep in on a Sunday morning. Well, the noise! Lawnmowers, weed-cutters, leaf-blowers, branch-mulchers, dirt bikes and gocarts roaring down the street, speedboats with huge engines roaring down the waterway, and on the playground nearby three whirring, screaming model planes. Have you ever heard a more horrendous, brain-frazzling sound?! And the cars! Bumper to bumper, honking, people hollering out the windows for others to move on. On a Sunday? On our bloody Day of Rest?!

I went for a walk and ran across a mall. It was noon. People lined up at the doors. I thought somebody was giving stuff away. Like hell. They couldn't wait to get in and spend money. There is something ugly about shopping on a Sunday. The mothers working in the shops, the kids missing that special meal. And all that junk being gobbled up. Aren't six days enough? Can't we give ourselves some peace at least on Sunday?

That afternoon I stopped and watched a ballgame. Kids as young as John Hardy was when he sat on the fence. My God. What a park! A real diamond, pitcher's mound, raked sand infield, real grass trimmed to perfection, padded bases, dugouts, benches, uniforms, kids with their *own* gloves, kid gloves for batting, hardhats. And bats. Man did they have bats! They had so many aluminum bats that if you melted them all down you could build yourself a plane. And yet everybody was as solemn as if somebody had just died. Anxious faces. Parents yelling, urging victory. Kids yelling dull slogans. Hustling. Throwing gloves in anger. Like a bunch of tiny, worried adults playing for their lives. The worst was when the kids in the field came in to bat. The coach called them into a huddle. Told them how they "got to stay aggressive, talk it up, shake 'em up, go in for the kill" because they had them "scared now," they had them "on the run."

What the hell was this? Was this a war or just kids playing ball?! Couldn't they wait until they grow up to have a bad time? Where was Eddy Emanoff? Where was John Hardy's sister? You might think I'm raving. Maybe I am. Maybe the years are coloring my youth. But I don't think so. I remember a lot of bad, but not on Sundays.

Then, you may rightly ask, what on earth has a ball-game got to do with the breakdown of our society or the polluting of the planet? Well, it seems to me, everything. And it goes far beyond the obvious, far beyond the sludge and smoke it took to mine, smelt, form and polish all those bats, weave and fabricate the uniforms, make the bleachers, bases, hard hats, gloves, and all. We've talked about this already with the toy. What is sad is that our kids need all this gear, cause all this pollution, just to go play ball. But what's even sadder, what breaks the heart, is that despite all the shiny gear, the perfect lawn, the bases, there wasn't a kid out there having any fun. Sure they played well, snapped that throw, showed hustle. But where was the joy? Where was the laughter? Where was that burst of irrepressible urge that made Dave Dowsett run after a fly ball and, after making the catch, without breaking stride, keep running down the street and vanish around the corner, leaving us all standing speechless,

19

without a ball? Then he came back a bit later from the fruit stand with a bag full of cherries.

We shared those cherries just as we shared the gloves and that old chipped bat. That's why we came. Not just to make a perfect throw, or beat the other guy—we played as hard as we could, really tried—but there was more. We came to be together, to be friends.

It didn't matter who played on whose team, or who hit best or who caught the best; it didn't matter how old you were, or if you were even—God forbid—a girl, and it didn't even matter if you were fat and slow. It would have been unthinkable to play a game without Eddy; the day would have been sad without his laughter.

So we played together and we sat around together, and learned to get along without parents, without coaches, on our own. We learned how to make each other laugh, and what would make us cry, and learned that if something hurt one of us it would somehow hurt us all. And I learned that you can use the same scruffy ball for four years and be happy, learned that you can have as much fun in desert boots as in spikes, and that all the shiny bats money can buy aren't worth one of my mother's Sunday meals.

Well then. If the flashy gear doesn't buy happiness then why have the damned stuff at all? And if something as small and innocent as uniforms and shiny bats can bring on such pressure and gloom, imagine how much sorrow a giant yacht can bring.

But anyway, back to Sundays.

On warm summer Sundays the family would go fishing. We would get into the old 20-horsepower Austin and putt-putt out to this creek about a half-hour from the house, grownups with kids, grownups without kids, who cared? It was a lousy place to fish. You'd catch a couple of catfishy things, and maybe a carp. But the hayfields were a nice place to lie, or you could kick a ball down on the bank, and the willows gave you shade, and in a bend there was a quiet bay, deep and warm, and the bottom mud would squish between your toes. We had fires and roasted bits of sausage and dripped the fat on a hunk of bread and made a fish stew with onions and paprika and everybody's fish thrown in. And lots of homemade wine. And we lay around and talked. We seemed to talk to each other a lot more in those days.

Of all the wonders North America invented, one seems to me among the most wondrous of all—the front porch. If you sat there long enough you could talk to the whole world. The neighbors drifted by and leaned on the fence and talked or sat on the steps and talked. And the guys would come and Ernie Flint would come and John Hardy's sister sat on the lawn and did her nails. And you could listen to Eddy Emanoff talk about his chickens, or to the baker talk about his wife, or you could tell your Mom about weird old Mrs. Kindler who filled up six blackboards in Biology and made you copy down every bloody word. Or you could just sit and watch the girls walk, or watch kids play, or park Granny in her rocking chair.

But times have changed a lot in thirty years. We shipped Granny off to some distant "Home," the kids are getting ulcers at the ballpark, Mom's at work, the friends are busy fending the yacht off the dock, and the neighbor waves to you as he rushes from car to house shouting "Hi there!" because he doesn't know your name. And all the front porches are empty. Or gone, replaced by forbidding two-car garages.

All this change didn't happen overnight. No great thing caused it, no evil willed it. It snuck up. It snuck up on us slowly over the years, a thoughtlessness here, a tiny neglect there; a bit too much ambition, a little too much greed. It snuck up on us slowly like our bad air, our poisoned waters, the dying cities, the dead seals. And what of the future? How much will things change now that our lives are so hurried and we have less time to care and much less time to think? And no Granny on the front porch to remind us of simpler times, better days.

We don't need statistics to tell us how bad our air has become; we can sense it. And we don't need numbers to tell us how our lives have changed; we can feel it. But it is worthwhile to look at a few numbers just to see exactly what has changed in the thirty years since we traded the front porch for garages and Granny for a VCR.

As most of us know by now the burning of fossil fuels such as oil, coal and natural gas has as its main by-product—aside from the desired heat—undesired carbon. In the old days we called it soot. It got on your hands and then on your pants and then your mother screamed and that was that. But now we find that the carbon that we see is just a tiny fraction of the carbon that we don't see—carbon that escapes into the atmosphere as gas. We as a society seem to be more efficient at producing carbon than we are at producing almost anything else: a whopping 5.6 billion tons in 1990 alone. And rising. Back in 1960 we produced *only* 3 billion tons. The U.S. output alone jumped 50 percent to 1.2 billion tons in that time, while Canada's actually doubled. The most frightening part is that this vast increase came about even as hundreds of our factories were closing, shipping much manufacturing, hence pollution, overseas. (Remember, these numbers do not include the pollution caused by all the things we import.)

To get an idea of just how much carbon 1.2 billion tons a year really is, compare it, say, with automobile production. The U.S. each year builds about six million cars at an average of about 1 ton each. So by weight, it makes about 200 times more carbon than cars. If you're still not impressed let me put it this way. To support the way we live, we North Americans must produce, *for each of us, every year,* five tons of carbon spewed into the air. That is an *increase* over the last generation of almost *one ton per person* in the U.S. and almost 1.5 tons in Canada. Now doesn't that make you feel just a bit ashamed? Or if you don't go in for shame, doesn't that make you feel just a little scared, if not for yourself then at least for your children? Anyway, the five tons of carbon per capita is the *good* news.

The *bad* news is that each ton of emitted carbon combines with oxygen to make 3.7 tons of carbon dioxide, so that our five-tons-per-person of carbon is suddenly eighteen tons, or the one-ton-per-person increase is now 3.7 tons. And the worst news is that it is this carbon dioxide—20 billion tons produced each year globally—that absorbs energy from the sun, creating what we now call the greenhouse effect, which most scientists now call global warming.

So there's the change. The next time someone asks you just how much the shiny bats cost, or the VCR, you can say without the blink of an eye: almost four tons of fresh

23

carbon dioxide . . . from each of us . . . per annum. Now do you believe the garage is filling up?

Maybe it's time we built a porch and brought ol' Granny home.

4

HOME?!

The dwelling-house was a substitute for the mother's womb, the first lodging, for which in all likelihood man still longs, and in which he was safe and felt at ease. —Sigmund Freud

Of all the old sayings America has given us, "There is no place like home," has to be the truest. We might admire castles and palaces but I think most of us would gladly trade them for a small house with a hearth. And almost no matter how exotic a place we travel to, the best part of every trip seems to be getting home.

Yet we seem to be unhappy with our homes. We decorate them, renovate them, add to them, replace what's old, antique what's new, in search of something—some feeling. When we can't find it, we move. We say we move because we need an extra room, bigger closets, a smaller yard; but is that really all? Or are we after something else? Something most of us are missing?

You might ask what this has to do with bettering either society or the world. Well, it seems that our homes are much more than four walls; they seem to be an extension of ourselves. And if we can discover what went awry with them, maybe we can discover what went awry with us.

Between the ages of five and eleven I lived with my grandmother and grandfather in Budapest in a tiny, cold-water flat. There was a stone-floored kitchen with a big wood-burning stove, an iron sink, an oilcloth-covered table, three chairs, and a glass-doored cupboard against the wall. The other room looked into a courtyard, had a bed in a corner where Grandfather slept alone because he snored, an enormous glazed-brick oven for heat, a doily-covered table full of family pictures, an old Phillips radio that gave a warm glow in the dark, and a pullout sofa where I slept with Grandma.

In the evening, when it got too dark to play outside, Grandfather would sip his wine while he taught me names of countries far away, and Grandmother would sew or make pasta to dry. When Grandfather's eyelids began to droop, Grandmother would get him into bed, then us to bed, and in the dark would give in to my pleas and tell me stories of her childhood in Transylvania. It was a good life. I asked nothing more from it than a real leather soccer ball.

Twenty-four years later in Vancouver, Candace and I built a house on the beach at the bottom of a cliff. Four stories high, with a footbridge to reach the driveway at the top, all glass and cedar with the ocean in front and the green cliff behind; three thousand square feet of architectural splendor that felt about as cozy as the Astrodome. After a year of shouting to each other from one empty floor to the next, we moved to Paris into a tiny ancient flat, where we felt comfortingly near each other; where we felt at home.

Why do we do this to ourselves? Why do we build huge, unused barns when all we want is the security of four walls and the warmth of another soul? Who is a house for? Is it to impress strangers, to make some poor passerby feel bad for an instant, or is it for us to spend our days in, feeling "safe and at ease"? It seems that just as we have lost sight of what was special about Sundays—friendships, solitude and calm—so we have lost sight of what was special about home—family, security and peace. And just as our Sundays have become not a day of rest, but a day to drag out and service all our gear, so our houses are no longer places that protect *us*, but instead *we* protect *them*; maintaining, paying off, repairing, servicing.

So what happened?

Not so long ago when you came of age and got ready to marry, you went to the end of the village, got the next piece of land, and, with the help of fellow villagers, built yourself a house to shelter you and yours. And that was that. Your house was yours. You could get on with your life, grow and raise what you could, help others when you could, get by, live in peace.

Not any more. Why? *Because the land is gone!*

It no longer belongs to your fellow villagers to give, but to the Ilaff-Ucry Development Inc., headquartered in Tokyo or Dallas. And while they won't help you build a little house, they will happily build one for you—as gargantuan a one as the bylaws let them. All you need to do is sign the "The Mortgage," the repaying of which will take you all your life. The price? $200,000 which, through a whimsical sleight-of-hand called interest, becomes $600,000 by the time you die.

Remarkable.

Remarkable that we gratefully slave away at mostly numbing, demeaning jobs for thirty years, paying off some thrown-together shack that any two of us could have built much better in six months, doing enjoyable, commonsense work like measuring, cutting, and banging in some nails.

When we were first married, Candace and I built a small house with our own hands. It was cedar inside and out, decks, skylights, oak floors, fireplace; all the comforts of home. Its size was humble, 500 square feet, but it had a living room, dining room, den, fully equipped kitchen, an airy loft-bedroom and of course a bath. It was as cozy a place as you could want. We built it in three months and it could have been even less had we not made the design so complex, hauled the material with a beat-up Porsche, and built in the dead of winter. Nevertheless, three months sufficed—with no previous experience— and it turned out nice enough to be written up in magazines and cost a grand total of—appliances included— $3000. Now granted this was twenty years ago; so let's double that for inflation to $6000; triple its size to give us room to swing the cat, $18,000; throw in a bit for extras and ease of figuring—and make it $20,000 even. And, to build the bigger house at a calm, leisurely pace, let us *quadruple* the time required to a year.

Now, compare this home-made house and the one you bought for $600,000. Simply subtracting $20,000 from $600,000 will give us a difference of $580,000. As for time, a $20,000 mortgage paid back at a similar monthly rate would be paid off in less than a year. Combine this with the year it took to build, and you have a difference of *twenty-eight years.* Now, no matter how forgiving a Christian you are, you will have to admit that you have been gypped out of an enormous pile of money, and that someone has picked your pocket of the best third of your life.

But where really is the difference? First of all, I have to add that the small house Candace and I built was a houseboat on pontoons that had cost $500, considerably less than the average lot. And herein lies *half* of the mystery—a broad rule of thumb says that half of what you pay goes toward the lot—because the question that keeps gnawing at me is: "How the hell can a piece of dirt that is too small to feed a goat be worth *14 years of a human being's life?*" The accepted excuse is that the price is high because, "This is a popular location, close to trains, planes, shopping malls and movies," but all that says is that it's a handy place to spend your life paying off the mortgage.

You will immediately protest that this is malicious phrasing because you do a lot more than just pay the mortgage while you're there; you go out to dinner, take in a ball game, go to the beach, pop in at the gym. True enough. But you do these things for minuscule bits of time to give yourself the illusion that paying off the mortgage is actually fun. Lumps of sugar. They're lumps of sugar to a tired old horse who spends most of his life pulling loads of wet coal across town.

But back to the lot. So society, through consensus of "location, location, location," has decided on land value. Yet land value is not established by us democratically. It is established by that teeny minority with much extra cash and incomparably less imagination who can think of no humane way to invest it, so they keep bidding up the price of land and houses. This is called land speculation. Now in a civilized society, utilizing unneeded cash *to drive the price of houses out of the average person's reach* would be pooh-poohed and discouraged by on-the-spot use of portable guillotines. Alas, in ours it is considered a wise investment, and those who excel at it get—instead of their head in a basket—their faces on covers of magazines. How long before we wake up and start filling those little baskets to the brim is anybody's guess, but until then we'll keep paying them and dozens of other extras who are part of a convoluted system that discourages simple, direct actions and thus separates us from a few hundred thousand dollars and our most energetic years.

For you will, on top of the land value, pay a realtor, lawyer, banker (with truckloads of interest), mortgage broker, bureaucrats (through fees, taxes, licenses and permits), and your friendly insurance man whom your banker insists you retain to protect "his" investment in case someone walks across it, drops dead, and sues your ass to kingdom come.

All this instead of just walking to the end of the village, picking up a shovel and saying, "I build here."

You smile and say how simpleminded a dream this is, that in a complex, "civilized" society you need all this interference to keep order. True. But you have to admit that our world is not complex by nature; it is complex only because we have allowed our system to interfere and convolute it for us. You might also ask, "How would a simpler world be a better place?" Well. It seems to me that if there is one thing that causes the brunt of both social and environmental pain, it is *not* that we don't contribute enough to society, but that we contribute too much—too much movement, construction, destruction, fabrication, garbage, noise, and stink. All this because we are chained to a society with a billion rules, conventions, regulations, and laws which force us *all* to work infinitely more than we need to.

If, for example, you had built your own house and shortly had no more mortgage looming over you, I think we could assume that you would spend a lot of the twenty-eight years you saved just hanging out: fishing, hiking, knitting, zucchini-planting and black-berry-picking. Not only would these activities result in much less pollution than your neighbor's hijinks at the local steel mill, strip mine, or cadmium company, but you would, with so much time spent close to Man and Nature, develop a more reflective, more reason-able life.

And all the bureaucrats and interferers would then be on modest pensions, saving immeasurable pollution not only by eliminating the construction, cooling, heating and disinfecting of their premises, but also by depriving them of their sizable incomes, which they currently spend buying hyperpolluting toys from power boats to corpo-rate jets to relieve the boredom of their uncreative lives. Just think of the sense of freedom we would have with all of them off our backs. Even Freud, one of the great fans of "civilization," states emphatically that, "The liberty of the individual is no gift of civilization. It was greatest before there was any civilization."

But back to your humble home for 600,000 smackers. Now that we've accounted for the first half, let us take a look at the second. It is standard practice for a contractor to charge a fee of 20 percent on all material and labor costs. The other 80 percent goes to subcontractors, foremen, a little for materials and the rest for very high-priced labor; $13–$25 an hour for people banging nails or smearing paint, or sticking two pieces of pipe together and holding them until the glue dries. (None of this is meant to offend tradesmen, for whom I have great regard, but you must understand that they are merely humans who perform simple jobs that you and your dearest can learn in a few days with a little effort, a few threats of divorce, and a couple of quick visits to the emergency room.)

Now for the house itself. So this is your dream home. Fine. But how much does it really have to do with you? Did you have a single say as to where it should be set, which window should face the sunrise and which the harvest moon, how it should look, where the rooms should be, how big and how many? Not bloody likely. If you're lucky you might have had a word about the color of the rug. If to this you say, "It's just a house, who cares anyway?," then why the hell spend a quarter of a century paying for the thing?

Coming Home

Anyway, here you are, key in hand, life in slavery, drenched in buyer's regret, so we might as well look at what you got.

The first thing we set foot on is The Driveway. A thousand square feet of freshly hardened tar. Can you imagine what that cost in pollution to produce, transport, lay down and roller? And do you realize that you paid about three grand for that beauty? Now you say, "What's three grand? I clear that in a month." Precisely! That's the point! A WHOLE MONTH! Can you imagine that if you really had the choice, the freedom that every field-mouse, worm and bedbug has each day, of getting up when he wants, going where he wants, doing what he wants, you would actually *choose*, instead of fishing by a creek, sitting by the ocean, strolling on a mountain path, you would *choose* to get up at six every morning, shave-shower-chew-gobble-run, drive in hellish traffic to the stable, get in the harness, spend eight hours pulling, jerking, slipping in the stinking streets, slaving, worrying, sweating, ass-kissing, taking the bloody whip, looking over your shoulder begging for the day to end?! Can you imagine spending a whole month of your one-shot precious life doing that, just so twice a day, to and from the stable, your stupid car can roll on something black instead of something green?! Would you actually choose to do that given the choice, the freedom? If you would, count your cards. You're playing with a short deck.

Of course we seldom think of our consumption in such terms. We seldom consider how much of our lives we must render in return for some object we barely want, seldom need, buy only because it was put before us. We think only in dollars and cents, whether we can sneak in the monthly payments. And this is understandable given the workings of our system where without a job we perish, where if we don't want a job and are happy to get by we are labeled irresponsible, non-contributing leeches on society. But if we hire a fleet of bulldozers, tear up half the countryside and build some monstrous factory, casino or mall, we are called entrepreneurs, job-creators, stalwarts of the community. Maybe we should all be shut away on some planet for the insane. Then again, maybe that is where we are.

Where the hell was I?

The Driveway. So now that we've flushed down a month, let us move on to the next surprise. Just look at that thing! A veritable palace—windows, bright lights, great doors that open at the touch of a button; a Chinese village of thirty could live here in great comfort, but for us it's just a place to keep the car. And over the years, with interest and insurance, a new roof here, a new door there, you will come very close to spending $30,000. A full year in the harness, a year gone of the short life, just to house that big tin bucket in a place fit for a king. So what will it be: a year on the beach listening to the waves, sun-warmed skin, sucking on a coconut . . . or the garage?

The House

I can think of few things more comforting than the sight of an old cottage in a meadow. I can linger and dream for hours. Its size could be diminutive, its luxuries minimal, but there is something about it, its simplicity, its permanence, that is reassuring, warming. I think it safe to say that this is a universal feeling, so why then is our continent not full of cozy cottages for us all? Why are we burdened with empty bedrooms, dens, and bathrooms, and cavernous rec-rooms where even the dog won't wander because it's too lonely? Why is the average new home nearly 50 percent larger today—1900 square feet against 1350—than it was just twenty years ago, even with the size of families going down? How can we be dumb enough to pay mortgage, heating, cooling, lighting, insurance, maintenance and repair for space we never use? If you object and say your house is sensible, fine; let's have a look.

Entrance

This is important, granted—first impression and all— but it is best for muddy boots, walking sticks, coats and hats, so let's put a bench along the wall, add coat pegs, and a chest for shoes. A six by ten foot room will do no matter what your shoe size. Yet house ads often brag about a cathedral entrance. I mean Merciful Mary Mother of Jesus, who the hell needs a cathedral for their smelly shoes?!

We once went for Christmas cocktails to a house in Arizona, big money, big lots, driveways long enough to curve, a portico the size of the Parthenon, and inside the huge doors an entrance the height of Brunelleschi's Dome in Florence. In the distance was the curving staircase from *Gone with the Wind*, with the *entire* Phoenix Boys' Choir on it, Christmas caroling their pre-pubescent hearts out. A little later they vanished, and out came card tables, dice tables, roulette wheels, barkers and croupiers, and onward went the night celebrating the humble birth of Christ.

The rest of the house was in keeping. The Jungle Room, the Alpine Room, the Pirate Room, the Wild West, stuffed this, stuffed that. Schizophrenia unchained.

And the hosts, embarrassed eyes, cemented smiles and all—the Ceaucescus seemed happier going to the wall—talked about their work, their life, and how they felt the time had come for them to make a "statement." Their house was it. Now *here* was a couple in need of a cathedral ceiling—and regular professional care.

The Living Room

There is simply no other room in modern North America more misnamed than this one. How can we call slouching brain-dead on a couch watching colored dots flicker in a box "living"? How many days a year are our living rooms filled with passionate live conversation or bubbling laughter? When was the last time friends and neighbors drifted in and out and sat down for a glass of wine or a cup of coffee and discussed the ailments of the world, their lives or their zucchinis? And when was the last time the whole mob of nephews, cousins, uncles, aunts and grannies draped themselves over the furniture with the ease and soft boredom of family? Aren't these the things that we could honestly call "living"? Are these not the things that make us truly human, enrich our lives, make our house a home? If our living room isn't for being together, if it's not for "living," then what is it for? If it's made just for the box then that's a crime. A double crime. Why bother spending extra years in a numbing job just so you can run to the numbing-box and be numbed a little more? Wouldn't we have been better off if we'd left the poor patch of ground below in peace, planted a little grove so we could look out at some green, some birds, some reality?

Dining Room

Who needs it? Once a day—if all goes well—we sit down in this dullest of all rooms and have a meal. And what a meal? How many of us sit down to more than some mushed stuff from a package or, at best, something hurriedly thrown together from meats full of hormones, vegetables full of herbicides, and fruit sprayed with liquid wax? What a feast. *Bon appetit.* Truly worth having a room for that!

And how often does the family eat together anyway without someone being off somewhere practicing blowing or twanging something, or learning with great dedication to break bricks with his hands. Perhaps there are arguments in favor of this kind of life but we certainly don't need to build a room to celebrate it.

The Mechanized Kitchen

If there exists concrete proof of the monstrous load of bullshit the world has sold us under the guise of progress, then the modern mechanized kitchen must be it. I mean for example, what the hell exactly does a garbage compactor do?! It costs a lot, requires much raw material to make, takes up space, makes noise and burns up a lot of power. It also blows up bottles, stinks like hell, gives you a hernia taking it out, and makes garbage impossible to sort or decompose. All it really does is make garbage tighter. So what?! What's so bloody great about tight garbage?!

Then there is the electric can opener. In the old days we took a can opener that resembled a pair of pliers, clamped it on, gave it a few turns and, by God! the can was open. Apparently we were living back in the Dark Ages, for today a kitchen would be thought barbarous without a machine to open cans. Why? Were the six seconds of manual labor deemed too strenuous? Or too demeaning? Probably neither. The truth more likely is that we associate the little machine with progress, not only the world's but our own; a small indicator that our mediocre lives have somehow improved.

And while we're at it, what about the dishwasher? We deem this machine as vital as our organs. We had one in that glass house on the beach, and I could forgive that it cost five hundred bucks, took up the space of five drawers, and blew hell out of our electrical bill; but what annoyed me was the noise. As I sat down for a peaceful evening, the thing sloshed and churned and made vulgar sounds, so I had to read or think in the ambiance of the corner laundromat.

And another thing. If the dishwasher was invented to wash dishes, then why do I have to wash them *by hand* first? I pick up the plate, wipe it, rinse it, then load it in the machine. Now that's not exactly eating bon-bons. Not to mention pots and pans which you always have to do by hand. So what's all the excitement?!

I won't go into details about the hundred other gadgets, electric knives, deep-fryers, choppers, grinders, mashers, squeezers, whippers, snappers, pulpers and slashers, most of which sit long-forgotten in some cupboard. Let us just grant that the modern kitchen is beautifully designed and full of magical machines . . . But what happened to the people?

The Laundry Room

Excuse me for asking, but since when do dirty gaunchies need a room of their own? Part of the reasoning is so you can iron there, but nobody irons anymore, and who wants to iron alone shut away with a machine? Isn't ironing more fun where there are people to talk to? Then there's the dryer.

Not long ago back yards were alive with clean laundry dancing in the breeze. And hanging the laundry out and taking it in was a social act, a time for a backyard chat with your neighbors. But no more. Not only are clothes-lines forgotten in most places, but are actually *forbidden* in some for being unsightly. My God, what have we come to! A dog dragging himself along in convulsions, dumping a giant steaming load on the sidewalk or the lawn is deemed acceptable but clean clothes hanging on a line are thought disgusting?!

The argument of weather is just as sad. Clothes dry on almost freezing days. And living in the city is no excuse at all. Millions from Tokyo to Rome who could easily afford machines still hang clothes on balconies or lines strung between windows. And to those who say they don't want their clothes dried in dirty city air, well let me ask you—where do you think the air in your dryer comes from? Some secluded, pristine Rocky Mountain glen?

Anyway, a friend in Italy, educated, well traveled in Europe and the Far East, started laughing when I told him about a machine that dries clothes. He didn't believe me. He thought it was a joke. Why, he asked, would any sane person pay for a machine—that some estimates claim uses up 10 percent of our continent's total electrical energy—instead of using a string, the sun, and the wind?

I told him that in North America it was a matter of prestige; you didn't dry your clothes on a line because your neighbor might think you're poor. Sadly enough, *that* he understood.

What has become of us? What has become of us that we are constantly judged, or at least *think* we're judged, by what we can afford? How little do we count for as humans when we judge each other not by what's in our brains or hearts or souls but by how fancy are the gadgets in our house? Sure some may say that a dryer saves some time but the question that is never asked is "For what?" Time to stare a bit more at the tube? Time to flip through another magazine to find out which airhead said what inanity to whom? Is that really preferable to standing in the backyard in the sun getting a little air, moving your arms, chatting over the fence?

No. The sad truth is that we live by rote. We emulate the Joneses and they are emulating only God knows who. We stopped reasoning and questioning long ago. Maybe Darwin was wrong after all. Maybe we are not descendants of passionate, lively, family-loving apes, but of sheep, whose only noteworthy characteristic is that they love to follow.

A Family Kitchen

Once upon a time the kitchen was the center of life in every house, with its warm stove, its big table, its hundred magic smells, the many hours of the family together, making meals, eating, cleaning up, talking—about nothing, about everything.

In Italian the word "casa" stands for house, but in Tuscany it means a whole lot more; it means the kitchen, and that's the heart of the house. Our next-door neighbors, the Paoluccis, live on a small farm, a ten-minute walk from ours through a vineyard and an olive grove, or longer on the clay road that runs along the ridge. You enter their house up worn stone steps, through ancient wood doors, and turn into the kitchen. The ceilings are high, the thick stone walls whitewashed, the floor sagged uneven, the tiles worn round. An enormous fireplace covers half of a long wall. Its great brick hood is supported by brick columns and a beam, and below it, on the raised hearth—inside the fireplace really—are two benches where you can sit to be real close to the flames. There is an old marble sink, a wood stove, a gas stove, a couch and odd shelves. There are two old tables end-to-end, one with a marble top—ideal for kneading and rolling dough—, the other covered with oilcloth.

This is the place where the family lives. This is where Eleanora does her homework, where Carla, her older sister, sews or argues with her boyfriend, where their mother cooks and fills jars with stewed tomatoes, or thick plum jam, where their grandmother, Nonna, roasts the chicken in the wood-fired oven and knits wool socks for the family, where Paolucci sits with his craggy hands that grip like a vise, and sips his wine and talks about his animals, his grapes or the heat or the rain, or kids his daughters or welcomes his neighbors.

And this is where twice a day the family eats its enormous meals of soup or pasta, meat, salad, cheese, fruit, and of course wine. And everything is fresh from around the house. The vegetables from the garden, the pasta made by hand on the marble table, meat from the barn-yard, wine from the cellar.

So that's the Paoluccis' kitchen. It is also their dining room, their living room, and the place where they play cards. As far as I can tell, if they built themselves a yawning dining room and a great, spacious living room they would gain nothing at all. But they might lose something. They might lose each other's company. They might lose someone to yell at, or touch, or make them smile out of the blue. They might stop being as natural and unselfconscious as you can be only around people you trust. They might forget how to be tolerant of each other. They might, little by little, forget how to be a family. They might, unintentionally, imperceptibly, and perhaps irreversibly, grow apart.

5

THE HOME GARDEN

There are few things in life more wonderful than being out in the yard after a rain with the air full of the fresh smell of wet soil. A recent *Los Angeles Times* survey on favorite pastimes found over 60 percent of those questioned put gardening at the top. Our friends in big cities from New York to Milan concur; the most common aspiration of city dwellers seems to be to have a country house no matter how humble, almost no matter where, just as long as it's attached to a little piece of land. And it's seldom to play croquet or have tea parties on the lawn, but rather to get out on a Sunday morning, grab a shovel, and dig dirt.

The countryside around Siena is dry by the end of summer. The gently rolling hills, all old ocean bottom, are mostly bare, the wheat cut, the earth plowed; only vineyards and olive groves and woods of oak and elm break the brownness of the land. We were taking a Sunday walk on a dusty road, the warm, dry silence all around, and hadn't passed a soul for an hour—there were only ruins in this valley, crumbling stone farmhouses on hill-tops with old cypresses—when in the middle of a grove of olive saplings we saw a fit-looking man of about fifty, trim, in shorts and tennis shirt, hoeing happily around the trunks of every sapling, opening up the earth for the rain where the blades of the tractor hadn't reached.

He was a bright and cheerful man, the director of the Bank of Tuscany in Siena, we discovered, who loves tennis and soccer, but most of all he loves digging dirt. He proudly showed us around his rolling land, the patch of sorghum he planted just for the wild pheasants, the woods where he cleared the undergrowth at the foot of every poplar and hoed shallow troughs to drain away the water to create an ideal habitat for truffles; but most of all he showed us his grove of olive saplings, 210 in all, planted by his own hands the previous spring and—he pointed out with beaming pride—already on one, if you looked really close, you could see the first cluster of tiny, pale green olives. He talked about growing things—vegetables, figs, anything you can eat—but pointed once again at his tiny olives, and said, "When you see the first fruit come out on something you have planted, it is such a great—," he searched for words, "such an immense joy!"

Then there's the harvest. To try to compare rationally anything you grew with your own hands, that you planted, watered, nursed, protected from evil, watched grow and ripen every day, to try to compare that with some fruit or vegetable grown by mere mortals elsewhere on this planet is a hopeless task; theirs don't have a snowball's chance in hell. Yours, blemished and misshapen as they may be, will be sweeter, richer, have flavors never imagined, while theirs will be a watery, tasteless, barely edible pulp. I know it's hard to believe but I look forward all morning of each late-summer's day to the time when, just before lunch, minutes before I put the first bite in my mouth, I go out to the garden and pick the darkest, reddest tomatoes I can find. To bite into a homegrown fully ripe tomato with the warmth of the sun still in it, is—well, what can I say—"such an immense joy!"

Fresh peas rolling out of the shell, or radishes just uprooted full of all the flavors that they have drawn out of the earth, or the apricot that you watch for days on end waiting for that perfect, ripest moment when it's about to fall, when as you touch it, it tumbles into your palm, warm, soft, full of nectar, that first bite—good God— well worth waiting the whole year for.

But, sadly enough, few of our gardens have any fruits or vegetables that would fill our hearts with pride and our stomachs with the best Nature can give. Instead we have empty lawns that everyone hates to cut, barely anyone looks at, and the only living thing that ever sets foot on is the dog. And of course we have trimmed bushes, hyacentus this and laburnicum that, that are about as much use as the cathedral ceiling entrance and certainly no prettier than a pear tree or a plum. Why?

In many European countries—not to mention almost every land in Asia, the tiny yards around the house are jammed with every edible plant the soil and climate will support. From Hungary to France to Italy the gardens are abrim from fence to house—front, sides and back—with everything imaginable from peaches to potatoes, from sunflowers to grapes. Nothing in vast quantities, but every square inch is used to produce something you can eat.

It is our sad distortion of life, our flabbergasting emphasis on possession and luxury that must have brought us to this state. It seems that when we are ready to tell the world that we've arrived, up goes the big house, in goes the big lawn. Then we spend the rest of our lives spewing herbicides and pesticides—about four times more per area than we use to grow our foods—to maintain it in putting-green condition.

The idea of growing real food around our houses is stranger to us than eating an ant sandwich. It's as if some shame has come to be attached to hoeing soil, seeding land, nurturing fruit and plants to feed oneself and one's family directly from the labor of one's hands. But if the same man dons a suit, sells futures or builds atomic bombs and brings his pesticide-drenched, herbicide-riddled, wax-coated apples, nitrogen-gassed tomatoes and color-injected cherries from the local supermarket in a thousand plastic bags, tin cans and colored boxes, then he is a man to be respected, somebody normal.

Doesn't all this strike you as just a little strange?!

I made an informal survey of gardens in a neighborhood in Vancouver, an easy thing to do because most houses have back lanes. Vancouver has an ideal climate for growing things—(many consider it the ultimate garden city)—short mild winters, long mild summers, enough rain to refloat Noah's Ark, and very good soil; it was all forest loam a mere hundred years ago. The place I looked at was a nice middle-class neighborhood, houses priced around $200,000, all well kept, all with gardens both in front and back; plants, lawns, trees, the works. Out of the ninety houses I passed, only eight had what could be called a vegetable garden. In terms of garden space occupied in the neighborhood, the veggies took up less than 1 percent—while driveways, roads and garages took up 50 percent. Yet every garage I peeked into was loaded to the gills with garden tools and machinery and enough murderous chemicals to wipe out the whole neighborhood twice over.

For a comparison, let me cite the World Resources Institute 1988–89 report on Java, where flourishing home gardens dot the landscape in cities and small towns. The land is hilly here, sometimes steep, tiered or terraced often with much effort to make it usable for cultivation. The tiers are orderly and about the same from house to house. The top tier has coconut palms, the next one down mangoes, guavas and other fruit; the tier below that has starchy food plants, and the lowest has vegetables like eggplants and chili peppers. The report concludes, "The resulting multilayered plant structure makes maximum use of light and nutrients, moderates soil temperature and provides a plethora of edible and saleable plant products. In addition to growing crops, many Javanese raise—at home—fish, chicken and goats."

The food produced in these home gardens make up a sizable percentage of the food consumed in Java, as well as adding to the income of the families that produce it, accounting for 25 percent of the family income of the poor and almost 10 percent of the income of the prosperous. Home gardens also encourage much diverse experimenting both in species and in types. In thirty-six gardens the surveyors found an astounding 230 species and 39,800 plants providing an invaluable gene bank for the future. When you compare that to our standard North American garden—lawn, laurel hedge, and three wilting geraniums—you have to admit something here is lacking.

As with many other things, we don't need scientific proof and irrefutable numbers to tell us what is going on in our lives; we can sense it. Passing through our average suburb, we get much the same feeling as in a well-kept cemetery: predictability, almost no variety, and not a sign of life. But in a country of home gardens life is on a rampage; plants crowding, fruits bulging, colors exploding, a hundred shapes and heights changing every week, things flowering, maturing, being harvested, wilting, dying off, the autumn earth freshly tilled and waiting for the sprouts of spring, and everything you touch, everything you see, you can eat. And, just as important to their society, someone is out there planting, hoeing, tilling, in touch with the soil, with the cycles of nature.

Our lawns might be one of the best examples of our culture gone awry; of us struggling, toiling and polluting and getting precious little in return. The sad part is that at the same time we pay astronomical sums for barely edible, overprocessed, overpackaged food, transported to us over thousands of miles. The average bit of food in North America travels 1,100 miles; at the Paoluccis, 50 steps. Much of it we could have grown right in our own yard with much more joy and much less effort, pollution, and expense than it takes to cut, water, and fertilize the useless bloody lawn.

Of course we have a major stumbling block; as the German proverb says, "All beginnings are hard." The problem is who in any neighborhood will have enough sense and fortitude to be the first to dig up the lawn and plant in its place a lovely patch of spuds. You can probably do it under one of two conditions: if you're armed with enough facts to convince your gasping neighbors, or if you're totally demented and just don't give a damn. If you're unfortunate enough to be deprived of the latter, let me try and help you with the former.

There seem to be four excellent reasons to lay waste to the front lawn: to save some money, to eat well, to save much pollution, and to keep the family together and happy.

Economy

According to the National Research Council, which is part of the National Academy of Sciences in Washington D.C., the American family spends between 10 and 50 percent of their income on food. This broad range is created by the wide difference in annual incomes, so that the family with an income of under $5,000 spends as high as 50 percent while the family who earns over $40,000 spends no more than 10 percent.

With these figures before us, something stunning jumps instantly to mind. In the case of the poorest families, one would have to assume that the jobs they hold, to earn what comes to less than minimum wage, cannot be said to be of the dream variety. Parking cars, flipping burgers, scrubbing toilets are simply not high on anybody's wish list. So. If a full one-half of the earnings from these mind-dulling, spirit-crushing endeavors goes to pay for food, would it not make a lot more sense to cut the time spent on these careers in half and spend some of it planting and growing your own?

The roar will go up immediately that many of the poor have no yards in which to plant a garden, and my response to that is that it's time to change the world to make sure that they do. But more about this later.

The other objection will be that, if you tried, by and large, to eat only what you grew, then you would have to say goodbye to Quarter-Pounders, Coke, Twinkies and Jello in fifty different colors. *Thank you Jeezus!!*

On the other end of the earning scale the implication is still more stunning. I think we all agree that eating, besides being needed for survival, is one of life's great pleasures. Yet a high-end earning family needs to spend no more than 10 percent of its working hours to guarantee this never-fading joy. Well then. Why the hell, may I ask, is it in harness for the other 90? Now I know many of us say that we love our jobs, but then why do we spend so much time looking at the clock or dreaming for fifty weeks of a two-week holiday? And why are the lines interminable at the Maalox stands, the shrink's office, the bars? Why does every desk and purse contain Tylenol and Excedrin? And why do we dream of the time when we can retire and live in peace? . . . Just asking.

So anyway. If you grow much of your own food you will save yourself much money. I mean, come on! $3.69 for a pound of tomatoes, when one plant raised in a garbage can gives you twenty pounds! You might object and say that growing things to feed yourself will take interminable time but that just isn't so. Remember Thoreau kept himself nicely fed by poking around his garden a mere half-hour a day. Candace provides with about an hour's poking, but then she stands and looks around a lot.

Other skeptics will argue that they eat very little of either fruit or vegetables, which of course is understandable given the insipid produce sold at supermarkets. How can anyone be enthusiastic over lettuce and tomatoes when they taste almost exactly like the napkin? I used to have very little interest in eating produce until we moved to Paris and began shopping at a street market twice a week, and this enthusiasm did not bloom into a mania until we moved to Italy and Candace began to feed us from the garden. Once I was introduced to *real* fruit and vegetables, I not only began to *enjoy* them more, but began eating them much more frequently, abandoning junky, often horrendously expensive, snacks and substitutes that I had eaten in the past. In other words, my daily consumption of fresh fruit and vegetables went from about 10 percent of my daily total food intake to well over 50 percent in a very short time. It is thus easy to see how your savings from growing much of your own food can be infinitely greater than you might at first think.

And how much can we save as a society by bringing back the old victory garden? Well, for a start, we North Americans, who have elevated weight reduction to a national obsession, could save most of the $35 billion a year on diet programs and liposuction alone. How much additional could be saved in hospital bills for curing all the ailments caused by the eating of fats and junk foods, everything from heart disease to stroke to various cancers, God only knows. Thus, by switching to a much healthier, leaner diet—everyone from the National Academy of Sciences to the American Cancer Society recommends high-fiber, low-fat diets—which you tend to do when you grow your own food, the financial gains could be almost endless.

Eating Well

When was the last time you ate a real tomato? I don't mean the red-water-tasting kind, I mean one that explodes with a hundred flavors as you take a bite. If you haven't for a long time then that's sad, but what is even sadder is that while some of us can remember a real tomato plucked from a childhood garden, most of our children have grown up eating only imitations. And worse than not being able to eat the tomato we once loved is never having eaten a real tomato at all.

But how can we account for such a great difference in flavor? First we have to realize that in our culture fruits and vegetables are no longer grown for flavor but for looks. Most of us don't shop at farmers' markets where we are enticed by the vendor's cries to sample his sweetest or his juiciest, but in supermarkets where if we bit into an apple we would be given odd looks, or be called a thief. We are, in other words, expected to judge what we eat by looks alone. Hence produce is now developed just like movies; get our attention, the contents be damned.

Then there is the question of purity of our food. About 500 million pounds of pesticides and herbicides a year are poured on what we eat. Some of these toxins leach away, but some end up on your plate. Most of them do little else than make farming more profitable or protect the fruits' and vegetables' outer layers from being blemished. In other words, if you grew your own food you could exclude these toxic delicacies from your menu.

Some would shrug at this and say "So what's a little pesticide? And what if things don't taste as good as they could?" But it is not as simple as that. The flavor of the greens and fruits we eat is not merely an indulgent luxury.

It is just as connected to our lives and the world around us as the air we breathe or the water we drink. If we do not learn about, if we are not exposed to, the hundreds of inimitable flavors our fruits and vegetables can give us, then we will never be able to learn to love them. We will happily accept manufactured half-foods of horrendous smells, colors and flavors simply because they're more memorable than the flavorless, insipid fruits and greens available to us. So we will accept insipidness as a part of Nature. And if we have never seen or smelled the clear blue sky of a winter prairie or a summer mountain, then we will unquestioningly accept our filthy city air. If we don't know the thrill of a forest, then we will learn to accept our concrete cities. If we don't know how to be amazed by Nature, we will not learn to love her. That is why we should fight tooth and nail for the tomato, the tomato full of flavor, full of sun.

To Reduce Pollution

The way we cultivate, transport and process our foods results in staggering quantities of avoidable pollution.

Whereas home gardens are most often worked with non-polluting hand tools and use mostly organic fertilizers and simple non-chemical pest controls, store-bought produce is almost always grown on enormous farms (94 percent of U.S. farms are over 120 acres), all of them using enormous machinery and enormous quantities of chemical fertilizers, pesticides, and herbicides. These not only pollute our bodies by ending up in our foods, but cause vast amounts of indirect pollution during their manufacture, transport and application, and "increase health risks to agricultural workers, harm wildlife, and pollute groundwater."

Then there is the great God of this century—transportation. While it is true, as Freud said, that, "Motor power places gigantic forces at man's disposal . . . thanks to ships and aircraft neither water nor air can hinder his movements," we have to ask, "At what cost?" Remember the toy. Take for example a simple flight in a 747 across the Atlantic from Rome to New York. The amount of fuel required to move this behemoth across the ocean is 140,000 liters, or roughly 35,000 gallons. That comes to a whopping 100 gallons a head or about the same amount an average small car uses in six months, driving 10,000 miles. Six month's worth of your car's pollution into the atmosphere, not to mention the pollution involved in the construction and maintenance of the plane or the airports it uses.

Now what on earth does this have to do with growing your own tomatoes? Well. Since long-range transportation has become so common, local production of most fruits and vegetables, an extremely common practice only forty years ago, has virtually ceased. Thus the tomatoes you eat may come from Mexico, the lemons from Israel, strawberries from Australia and even the cut flowers you gave Mom for Mom's Day were likely flown in from Colombia. Since your weight and volume is not drastically different from a couple of sacks of lemons, you can readily deduce the amount of pollution involved in their transport.

Part of the blame lies in the demand for residential land, hence skyrocketing land costs near urban centers. In the past, most cities were surrounded by truck farms and orchards which fed their populace. But no more. The great fertile valleys from San Diego to Los Angeles are gone, replaced by subdivisions with herbicided lawns. The citrus groves of Florida and the truck farms of the Northeast, South and West fared much the same. So our food is shipped the mentioned 1,100 miles, each and every bite. This long-distance madness has to stop. A World-watch Institute report speaks wistfully of a sustainable world of the future, warning of devastated economies and unliveable environments if we continue as we are. That sustainable world, which has cut its carbon emissions to one-third of today's, "cannot be trucking vast quantities of food . . . thousands of kilometers." Amen.

Then there is the processing and packaging. According to the National Academy of Science, a farmer receives only twenty-five cents of every food dollar spent. In other words, if you were to amble down to your neighborhood farm (were they still in existence) and buy most of your edibles direct, you would save yourself 75 percent of your food bill. Where does this 75 percent go? Pollution. I know you're sick of it but let's stay with the tomato. At the farm your tomatoes are boxed, trucked to a wholesaler, then to your retailer, where all too often they are repackaged into ozone-killing, hence skin-cancer-causing, Styrofoam trays, then covered with cancer-causing shrink-wrap. Then they are put into a refrigerated display case drenched in lights and music and promoted by tons of junk mail that's dumped on your doorstep. Now, you jump in your huge steel crate pulled by 150 horses, grab the three tomatoes in their deadly tray, and have the 150 horses pull you home again. Bravo!

But this is kid's stuff compared to what happens if you buy a can of tomato sauce instead. Imagine machinery bigger than a house that peels, mulches, presses, crunches, boils and filters your defenseless tomato. Don't forget the iron ore mines and the smelters and the steel mills making cans, the logging camps, the pulp mills, paper mills and printing presses churning out the labels. All this ruckus, all this toil, all this devastation, instead of taking ten steps to your garden, ten steps back, and boiling the tomato in a bloody pot.

So if you add up all this pollution, you will readily see how you are contributing to the global nightmare by not growing as much of your own food as you can. At the same time you will understand why a pound of tomatoes can cost $3 at the store instead of the three cents to grow in your own garden.

It is true that eating only locally grown food would restrict our diets because even the most honorable intentions will not sprout oranges in North Dakota; some transportation of some things is unavoidable. But these are not the major culprits. The culprit is our spoiled-brat insistence on eating strawberries in November, apricots in January and apples in the spring. Most of you will say "Well, what's wrong with that?" Nothing. Except that none of the above-mentioned fruit grows in the northern hemisphere at the above-mentioned times, so the strawberries fly 10,000 miles from Australia because Ralphie in Manhattan wants to have them for brunch tomorrow with his clotted Devon cream. Would bloody Ralphie have a bloody coronary if he ate strawberries only at the times they grew within a thousand miles of his bloody little house?! Hardly. He might instead have the great pleasure you get from expectation, from waiting, a semblance of that special joy you feel on Christmas morning. The potential for this joy is lost when we can have anything we want anytime we want it. As Freud said, "What we call happiness in the strictest sense comes from the—preferably sudden—satisfaction of needs which have been dammed up to a high degree, and it is, by its nature, only possible as an episodic phenomenon." Or, as Goethe said, "Nothing is harder to bear than a succession of fair days."

And growing your own food yields pleasures beyond the palate. Who is to say that the daily joys of watching the seed sprout, the tree grow, the flowers bloom, the fruit swell and ripen, are any less profound than the eating of the fruit? I remember when we built the big house on the beach. Every day we worked from dawn 'til dusk. When the others left I stayed, put away the tools and the cuttings, cleaned up, swept up, then sat down in a corner in the twilight with the dark sea at my feet, and stared at the long day's work, stared at beams or joists or siding we had set in place that day. Those were special times. I don't remember times like that once the house was done.

To Hold Together the Family

When we first came to Canada we lived in an attic with a mandarin orange crate hung out the window for a fridge. Near us lived my stepfather's far-removed relative whom I called Feribacsi, which meant 'Uncle Frank.' Feribacsi had a place that even in retrospect seems like paradise to me. Not long before, the whole valley around him had been small farms with lots of geese and ducks and turkeys, and across the road from his house a chicken farm still lingered, where you could take your battered egg carton and come back with it full of eggs, some still warm, some covered with bits of straw sticking to the shell.

Feribacsi lived in a small one-bedroom house with his wife Ildiko. It was surrounded by flowers and always perfectly kept. But it was the two acres of land around the house I really loved. There was a small lawn, an orchard, a vegetable garden, an overgrown field, and in the back, woods, with a great abandoned bramble-covered chicken coop. Many years before there must have been a small clearing behind the coop because there were no trees there—only waves of brambles that climbed the coop walls and poured in through the windows. One Saturday evening Feribacsi announced that if we wanted to have our own vegetable garden, the bramble-jungle was ours.

We started hacking early Sunday morning. My step-father was in the lead, wielding a machete, my mother right behind him tugging endless brambles with a rake, and me close behind with a little army shovel whacking away at berry roots that went all the way to China. For a week, every evening after work, out we went behind the chicken coop, picked up our weapons and attacked. My stepfather hacked and crushed the mess, then with a great crowbar tore out the roots. My mother, though she'd never touched a tool bigger than an egg beater, yanked the broken bits as if it were her vocation, piled them in a great heap, then set them all on fire, while I with my shovel and a bucketful of water stood an ardent watch, making sure we didn't burn the whole world to the ground.

It was late in May. The evenings were long. There was still light in the sky as we walked home along the dusty road back to the attic every night, tired as dogs but often in stitches over my attempts at yodeling like Gene Autry. We slept well. It took us two weeks of cursing, sweating and yodeling to clear out the bramble and tear up the bloody roots. Then we turned the soil. My God, what soil it was! I was only eleven then and knew nothing about humus or soil richness and not a damned thing about growing things, but there was something about that thick black forest loam, the feel or the smell or how it crumbled in your hand. Then we laid out the plant beds nice and straight, each as wide as a pick handle was long, then we stomped down the paths to keep the weeds from growing, my mother and I with our shoes and my step-father with a round of alder that he'd made a handle for—the earth shook under us as he thudded that thing down—and then on the tenth of June, three months to the day after we set foot in the New World, we seeded the damp, black soil of our almost-own piece of land.

For a week nothing grew. We watered the barren soil every night, then walked home. I never said a word, but I had great doubts that anything would ever come out of that empty dirt. Then Saturday it happened. It was hot. The sun was high, the sky clear, and by late afternoon the woods around the empty dirt breathed a fragrance I had never smelled before. I was near the garage, helping Feribacsi wash his maroon Ford for the Sunday drive, when a joyous cry from the chicken coop cut the air. We ran. My stepdad and my mom were kneeling on the ground, their faces low, yelling "Look, look!" I thought the empty soil had finally driven them mad. But I looked anyway. I squatted by the beds and tilted my head side-ways and saw in that barren earth, in the light of the falling sun, standing in straight rows like miniature sol-diers, delicate green somethings reaching toward the sky.

It was a good summer. Dennis Mitchell and I made a fort in a hollowed stump; in the evenings we watered and weeded our garden that by August was as lush as Tarzan's jungle; on Sundays we went fishing in the creek, and, to the irrepressible joy of the whole family, I completely and forever lost my urge to yodel.

By the first day of school the afternoons cooled and the lettuce no longer grew, the peas no longer ripened. The weeding stopped and the watering stopped, but three times a week we were back behind the coop harvesting corn and green and yellow peppers, digging up potatoes, parsnip and onions, cutting down dead stalks of flowering Brussels sprouts or just sitting on the coop's steps, still warm from the sun. Even on October evenings when the streets were empty and every TV glowed with the first hockey game of the season and the brambles had begun their fresh attack, the garden held us together—not behind the coop but in the kitchen of the attic. We canned.

That piece of barren dirt had provided enough food for a whole army and what we couldn't eat—most of it—we canned. Those evenings the kitchen looked like a greenmarket run amok. Piles of peppers and cabbage, tomatoes and dark gherkins lay about. Knives flashed gutting peppers, shredding cabbage, slicing beets, nipping the ends off green beans and peeling little onions; Mason jars boiled in great pots on the stove, lids were scrubbed, and rubber rings replaced. A big shelf was made of splintery planks in the coolest corner of the attic to house the rows of jars full of all the colors and flavors you could name. And all through the winter months and on into the spring the garden remained with us. It was there with every dinner each time a jar came open with a pop, each time we crunched a pickle. It was there as clear as a summer's day with, "Remember that damned shovel," or "that huge pumpkin" or "that slug." It was there in the muddy spring on the cleaned-off kitchen table with the colored bags of seeds and carefully pencilled plans of all the beds with so much laid aside for this, so much for that.

The vegetable garden held the family close for years; behind the coop, then behind our own tiny house, then later behind the bigger house we built. But somehow with each place, with each year it grew smaller, and somehow with each place, with each year, we grew apart. The only meals we shared in those last years were on holidays. And there was just a row of parsley left the year my mother died.

Whether abandonment of the garden was a cause of the rift between us or just a symptom, who can say? But in those gardens there were special moments; a lot of good ones and probably more bad than I remember. But whatever else those gardens gave us, they gave us common ground. My mother had her own job and my stepfather had his and I had school and friends and sports, and we all had our own problems, needs, sleepless nights and fears, but in that garden we shared and shared alike, loved it and hated it, harvested and worried and weeded, all together. Perhaps that's not much. But in a world as chaotic as ours, where the ties between us loosened long ago, isolating parents, isolating children, giving us so little in common to share, then, at least looking back, that garden seems an island remote from senseless struggles, where not only could we shut the world out, but we could shut ourselves in, together and alone.

6

THE MYTH OF
THE STEADY JOB

*And I fell to thinking of my silent, backstreet, basement
office, with its obliterated plate, rest-couch and velvet
hangings, and what it means to be buried there alive, if
only from ten to five, with convenient to the one hand a
bottle of light pale ale and to the other a long ice-cold filet
of hake. Nothing, I said, not even fully certified death,
can ever take the place of that.*
—Mr. Rooney, from *All That Fall*, Samuel Beckett

I got my first summer job when I was sixteen and badly
wanted a bicycle. My friend Glenn Dick worked in a
small furniture factory for 60 cents an hour, and that
sounded good to me, so off I went through the wood-
chip-littered yard and got hired. The factory was in a dim

half-basement with light filtering through tiny sawdust-covered windows, and a bit more from a few sawdust-covered bulbs. The air was a blizzard of formaldehyde and dust. The noise was beyond deafening. Sawblades screamed and planers whined and routers howled as they tore and gouged the rock-hard pressboards, spewing dust, glue-shrapnel, and stink.

There were five of us in that little shop cutting up boards of glued-together sawdust, covering them with wood-grained plastic and making them into beds. We communicated by shouting into each other's ears, or with hand signals, or not at all. At lunchtime they shut off the machines and turned off the dusty bulbs and we went out into the little yard, sat on piles of boards and quietly ate the lunches we had brought wrapped in wax paper from home. We didn't talk. We were grateful for the silence.

The foreman was a squat Pole in a glue-caked apron who had the exuberance and energy of a Turkish whirling dervish. He was everywhere at once; bursting from the clouds of dust, dashing among the blades, diving into the gloom, roaring unheard in the din—his bare arms waving, tugging, as if waging war against the murderous air, the maddening noise, the world. He had been there four years. He was saving up to open a little nursery to raise trees. At night he went home and blew sawdust into handkerchiefs.

I tried to imitate him. I tried with all my heart to rise to the challenge of the job. When that didn't work, I tried pretending. I wrapped a dotted kerchief around my face and pretended the boards were gold bullion; handled them with great finesse like Yves Montand handled nitro-glycerin in *The Wages of Fear*; tried to pretend we were outwitting screaming sci-fi monsters; eight hours a day I tried pretending the dust was fog, the noise music, tried to tell myself that this hour buys a bicycle chain, the next hour buys the brakes, tried to make sense of it all, tried to count the minutes, tried to sing, tried to laugh. But nothing worked. I'd look up and see the sawdust-covered bulbs.

Leaving at night didn't help. The stench of the formaldehyde came with me in my skin, the roar stayed in my ears, and even after a bath and dinner I could not shrug off the feeling that for eight hours I had been reduced to the lowliest form of life, locked in a place so foul that, if I had been a dog, the Humane Society would have come to rescue me—with sirens.

I quit after a week; something in me wouldn't let me go back there again.

Next, I went caddying on a golf course by the sea. My God! Sun, rolling hills, little lakes, rows of trees, sky, all the fresh air you could breathe, and silence; only birds and wind and the whipping of the clubs and the whack of the little balls. You went for a stroll through a meadow and someone paid you for it. A bloody miracle! Sure you packed the clubs but they weren't all that heavy, and you could always change shoulders or put the bag down while they putted, or even lean on it when nobody was looking. Then there were the carts. Paradise. Bloody paradise. Once in a blue moon, if you were really lucky, you'd get some guy who was too lazy even to pull his cart, and then all you had to do was stroll along with the two-wheeler behind you, stop now and then, pull out a club and watch the other poor saps sag under their loads. That's when you took a deep breath and thanked God for having let you die and come straight to heaven.

The only bad part was that the people you worked for thought you were made of air. They chatted among themselves, laughed, smiled at each other, then came to get a club and looked through you at the sea. At first I didn't mind. I was happy enough just to be outdoors, happy to be stashing away my four dollars a day. I put down being ignored to people's natural shyness. But as the weeks went by and I got the same groups time and time again, I began to admit that it was something else. It wasn't shyness that made them not introduce themselves when they first met you, and it wasn't shyness that turned their eyes away when they handed you the clubs, or walked away without a word when they handed you the money. They had fulfilled their obligation; they had paid. And no more was required.

I fantasized a lot while carting around the clubs, but this time not about being somewhere else. This time I fantasized about real things near me—about pushing their little carts to the bottom of the lake, or hanging the fat-toad doctor's bag in the highest tree, or braiding all the lawyer's clubs into shiny pretzels. Now you might think me hostile or even violent for those thoughts, but I swear I was as gentle as a lamb—never even flipped a garbage can on Halloween for chrissake—but I'm sure that deep in all of us glows a spark of rebellion, and this is fanned, as it should be, when we are reduced by others to ignored beasts of burden. I emphasize 'by others' because for myself, for my own house, my own land, or to help my neighbors, I'll happily be the lowest draft mule of them all. I'll haul rocks all day, pile bricks, chop wood, shovel pig shit by the cartload, or with the Paoluccis load ninety-pound bales of hay on top of a ten-foot stack in hundred-degree weather all morning and after lunch (better after lunch when you're full of pasta, roast duck, and wine), but somehow that's all different; you might still be a draft mule but you're a draft mule on your own. And when you're a draft mule on your own, you can at least limit your muling to honorable work like putting a roof over your head, or food into your mouth, or hay into your shed for the animals for winter, instead of packing stupid golf clubs for some half-dead horse's ass, whose only aim in hiring you is to show his golf pals that he can afford a mule.

And maybe the best part of muling on your own is that you can be as alive as you damned please. You can laugh or bray or sing your heart out, or yell until your lungs burst, or dance around like a damned fool or lie down under a tree. It's up to you. You're free. Every minute. As free as you would be on your yearly two-week holiday if you could still remember what being free once meant.

Most of you might dismiss this as the raving of some idealist who simply doesn't fit into the modern, well-ordered world. That's probably true. But where exactly do you yourself fit in? Where and when in this world do you feel wildly happy? Or truly free? Or fiercely alive, or at peace, or even just content? I don't think these emotions are an extravagant luxury. I would think them to be the norm among a species that trumpets itself superior to all others in both intellect and spirit. I would think them the norm in anybody's life, and if they're not, then perhaps he doesn't fit into this world any more than I. And if, as it seems, so many of us live without experiencing these emotions, living the life of a restless drone, if so many of us qualify as Freud's 'civilization's discontents,' then perhaps it is not we who don't fit into this world, but it is this world that does not fit in with us.

And if this is true, then perhaps it's time we stop changing ourselves to death. Stop changing jobs, cars, houses, wives and husbands, the color of our hair, the size of our thighs or our bank accounts. None of these have worked together or alone. And if all this self-changing has brought no lasting joy, then why do we believe that the next one will bring salvation? Maybe it's time to leave ourselves alone. Maybe it's time instead to change the world.

You would think that with our much-flaunted technology and knowledge, we could create a society that could satisfy the basic physical and emotional needs of its members. Yet very few discussions today contain long-term plans regarding *us*. Attention goes instead to rapacious myths and monstrous institutions, both deemed by those in power to be of infinitely greater import than mere people. Priority goes to the military, whose major task is finding bogeymen to justify its astronomical spending; to giant corporations that expand and devour for no better reason than to keep from being devoured themselves; myths like National Security and National Interest, which are cited every time someone's pal abroad loses money and we do something vile to help him out; that great holy The Economy, whose expansion is said to trickle down to us poor saps below; and our Grail, The Steady Job, held to be the sure way to the American Dream. All of these bear a frightening resemblance to what we escaped from in Hungary in 1956, only there it was called The Communist State, whose success was guaranteed to bring happiness to its citizens, even if it killed them.

The Steady Job is certainly the most tempting of the above myths. And why not? It sounds risk-free, lucrative, and promises not only eternal bliss but also all the wonders of the mall. And yet its worst crime is not that it misleads—it is only steady until you're laid off, and for the last twenty years has not even kept pace with inflation—but that it excludes; pre-empts the option to lead an independent, varied, and truly secure life. Yet it has become the lifeblood of our system. We even manipulate our children toward it from an early age. Seemingly innocuous questions like, "What will you be when you grow up?" imprint on vulnerable, impressionable minds that in our culture merely being human is a waste of time, but being a truckdriver means a lot.

So, instead of recognizing our burning desire for security, love and friendship, and working full time at satisfying them *directly*, we pour all our energies, both physical and mental, into training for, finding, and clutching a Steady Job; our one-shot magic potion toward fulfilling all our needs. This is not only putting the cart before the horse, it is more like putting it right on top of her. Wouldn't it make infinitely more sense to put our hearts and souls—and hands—into building ourselves a home, getting by, finding a lover, and finding good friends, while working full-bore at becoming the wisest, kindest, wittiest, most creative human beings we can be? *Then*, if the urge moves us, *only then*, we would go out and get a Steady Job.

I think we all agree that most of our Steady Jobs are emotionally stifling, and DULL!; if not quite as close to "certified death" as Mr. Rooney's, then not too bloody far. How stifling and dull there is no need to describe. We have all had them and wished to hell we didn't but I do think it worthwhile to look at just how *un*-steady Steady Jobs really are.

William Kolberg and Foster Smith, president and vice-president of National Alliance of Business, drew a frightening picture of the average blue-collar male American worker's career in the past twenty years:

1. Bored, he leaves school at seventeen to take on a full-time job at the fast-food joint where he has worked part time for two years. Earns minimum wage plus fifty cents an hour. No health benefits.

2. For eight years he drifts from job to job looking for better pay. At age twenty-five—based on maturity, not skill—he earns $6.25 per hour.

3. He marries at age twenty-six. Realizes that he needs a skill to earn more. Takes classes at community college or technical school.

4. At twenty-eight, finds semi-skilled job paying $8.75 an hour with full benefits.

5. At thirty-eight he survives company cutbacks and, through on-the-job training, he has learned to run high-tech machinery and earns $13 an hour.

6. At forty-eight, he is laid off. His company has retrenched.

7. With his rarefied skill non-transferable, he uses up his unemployment benefits. Takes job as security guard for eight dollars an hour. His wife gets job at department store to make ends meet.

Not an illustrious life cycle for a noble human being.

And it has been much the same for the last 140 years, during which the promise of steady jobs has lured us into the cities from small towns and family farms. As recently as 1850, nearly *ninety* out of a hundred North Americans lived in the country, but by 1990 that number shriveled to *two*. Sporadically, between recessions, depressions and wars—almost always started in big cities—the promise was made good. For thirty years after the Second World War, life in the city boomed and we partied. Family income, after inflation, doubled, as did the number of cars sold every year. Court cases and divorces doubled too, but when you're having fun who frets over details? So we bought whatever we could grab, *quintupling* the amount we spent on cosmetics, recreation, and toys. Economic prosperity seemed as if it would never end. Then it did.

Starting in the Seventies, the road to paradise took a short-cut to hell. Between 1972 and 1992 wages adjusted for inflation *fell* 20 percent. It is true that family income climbed a paltry 1 percent, but then 40 percent more married women are working, and the average work week has *lengthened* 8 percent in twenty years. (So much for the promise of "progress" giving us more leisure time.) The only lasting boom we have had since has been in the amount of pollution, the numbers of the homeless, and those of the very rich. Between 1970 and 1989 the number of Americans with incomes of a million dollars or more a year increased from 642 to 61,987—nearly a *hundredfold*. And we had a veritable windfall in the rise of vicious crimes; since the mid-sixties murders doubled, robberies quintupled, aggravated assaults, rapes, and the salaries of corporate CEOs quadrupled.

There were some never-to-be-forgotten corporate-sponsored days in the early Nineties that taught believers in steady jobs lessons in cruel reality. Xerox announced a 20 percent trim of its white collar jobs; Sears Roebuck a 33,000 job cut over two years; IBM said it would cut 20,000 more jobs in a year in addition to the 65,000 it had eliminated since 1986; banks and S&Ls slashed 50,000 jobs in a single year; and General Motors, instead of the normal annual bonus, announced on December 18, 1991 the permanent termination of 70,000 longstanding positions. Merry Christmas! One laid-off bank vice president, whose banker wife was also experiencing the falling ax, summed up the stunned reaction of the country in the *New York Times*, "Can you believe it? We both got into this thinking we were set for life."

Our faith was dealt further blows by an avalanche of bankruptcies of corporate cornerstones from Pan Am and TWA to S&Ls and Macy's. The layoffs that accompanied these were just a part of the economic devastation. As the *New York Times* wrote, "When Pan American World Airways went bankrupt in December . . . more than 20,000 retirees and their dependents were suddenly left without health benefits. . . . A General Accounting Office study (1991) of 40 troubled companies found that nearly half ended benefits for some 91,000 employees. Nine million retirees are enrolled in health plans that could be terminated." Some, who had dedicated their whole lives to companies in hopes of retiring to peace and security, found themselves without health insurance and were forced to sell their homes to be able to afford insurance on their own.

Yet what is often more damaging than the actual dollar losses incurred during such upheavals is the sense of uncertainty even among those working. In emotional terms, being laid off is only slightly worse than the nagging dread that you might be next to go. I remember our first years in Canada, when my stepfather was forced from job to job. He had been a landscape architect in Hungary, but in Canada he had to begin by digging ditches, planting trees. In the winters it rained. The ditches turned to mud. He was laid off. By late fall the family had the jitters. We listened to weather forecasts, watched the skies, and prayed. And fought. About eating expensive meat, and who left the door open and let out costly heat, and how could we bear the shame of neighbors watching while the repossessers hauled the TV down the stairs. And between the fights was the silent shame on my stepfather's face because he, an intelligent, educated man, no matter how hard he worked, no matter how he tried, had somehow failed; was unable to guarantee his family food on the table or a roof to eat it under. There are few things sadder than watching an able man in the prime of life sit helplessly, numb with worry. The repossessors never came—my mother paid the bills cleaning people's houses—but for how bad we felt they might as well have carted off the bloody lot. During some of those nights, sitting there among all the things we had, but didn't own, it seemed as if spring would never come.

As Louis Bromfield wrote, "The high standard of living in America is an illusion, based upon credit and the installment plan, which throw a man and his family into the street and on public relief the moment the factory closes and he loses his job."

The dread of losing one's job and being unable to provide has, by now, crept into most of North America's homes. It was reported in most major journals that during 1991 one out of five workers was at one point unemployed. That many were rehired or found new jobs did little to repair the damage, for much of the re-employment was often lower-paying or part-time work with few or no benefits. And over eleven million don't even have that.

The stories were endless. One man, the vice chairman of an electronics firm, had a sprawling home, two condos, two Cadillacs, Arabian horses; the American dream in spades. Then his firm closed. Little by little he lost the house, the condos, the horses, then the cars. He now works at Sears, selling aluminum siding, and feels lucky to have a job.

The most shocking one was on National Public Radio, the story of a highly respected computer programmer, laid off after twenty years. He had sent out over 400 resumes to no avail. Yet the myth of the steady job goes on. It is still the keystone of the American dream and on it depend the others: the split-level, the appliances, the car. And now, after years of a shrinking economy, people all over North America are losing the keystone and some, within a few months, when the savings run out, watch the whole dream crumble.

And the national uncertainty creeps on. A November '91 *Newsweek* poll found identical fears running through the minds of a great number of Americans. Almost 65 percent worried about having enough savings for retirement, and, more immediately, paying medical or health costs. More than half worried about maintaining the life they have, while almost half feel uncertain about being able to repay loans and finance their children's education. And as many dread the major wage earner in the family losing a job. And judging by the massive layoffs in recent years—layoffs that most experts say will be permanent as companies become leaner and meaner still—their worries don't seem irrational at all.

Robert Harrington, after twenty years on the job at a telephone-book printing company, was laid off last July and lives on unemployment. He and his son gave up a large colonial home and moved to a small apartment. Rick Anderson, 40, a coal miner, was laid off from the mine where he had spent the better part of a hard, hard life. And what is even more disturbing, more inhumane than being discarded like an old shirt in the prime of life, after having sacrificed most of it for one company, is *how* the layoffs are being done. Gary Castellan spent most of his working years in a giant steel mill for LTV Corporation. In the early 1980s he was let go, only a few months before he would have qualified for a pension. "They made sure we didn't get it," he said. Of course not all dismissed employees are treated as shabbily as Mr. Castellan, who was costing the company $11 an hour. Mr. F. Ross Johnson, who was chairman of RJR Nabisco until three years ago, stepped aside after losing a takeover battle for the company. He was given a nice sendoff *and $53 million*. Meanwhile due to the debt incurred in the battle, 2,600 less illustrious employees were dumped.

Just last year, Roger B. Smith, the CEO of General Motors, who ran the company to recordbreaking losses during the 1980s, waltzed off into retirement with a pension of $1.2 million *a year*! But the most disturbing part was that this pension was raised more than 50 percent only months before GM's Christmas Special, which blew 74,000 jobs permanently to the moon. That 74,000 soon-to-be-terminated are not singing in unison, "A tisket a tasket let's fill that little basket" shows the exemplary benevolence of 74,000 souls.

Of those still clinging to jobs, almost 80 percent saw their dream of growing affluence grind to a halt years ago. Michael Storm and his family, of Peoria, Illinois, are a good if sad example. He is earning $45,000 a year making transmission housings at Caterpillar Inc. But, as is true of 80 percent of the nation's households, the Storms' earnings have not gained ground on inflation since the early 1970s. That means he has to work extra hours to make the payments on the car. And it also means that the two-bedroom starter home he bought when he got married 16 years ago is looking more "forever" every day. The only thing that has changed is that the two bedrooms are now occupied by his four children, and he and his wife sleep in the living room—on the couch. And Michael Storm and his family, with Caterpillar's continued automation, are expecting a layoff any week.

Millions of others like John Gillson, 58, and his wife Laura, 57, continue to work and worry. He is an engineer, she a computer programmer who lost part of her retirement benefits in the collapse of Executive Life Insurance. They feel they are barely hanging on. "We're sitting around waiting to be laid off," she said. Or as Julia Carlisle, laid off by CBS News, bitterly said, "We learned an awful truth—that we are expendable."

We seem to be caught on a runaway train of a system which anthropologist Colin Turnbull described as one of "cutthroat economics, where almost any kind of exploitation and degradation of others, impoverishment and ruin is justified in terms of an expanding economy and the consequent confinement of the world's riches in the pockets of the few." Why the system goes on without people yelling "Enough!" is perhaps our greatest mystery. Maybe my friend, old Mr. Bradley from Pender Island, was right when he said, "We are all asleep while the world slips from under us."

That a change is needed is beyond doubt. How profound a one is hard to say, but as B. Drummond Ayres in a *New York Times* essay concluded, "What remains is a nagging doubt about the strength and viability of American capitalism and, for that matter, the viability of the whole American system of government."

7

HUMANE CORPORATIONS

There is a scene in an old John Ford movie in which Oklahoma sharecroppers are being evicted from the land their families had worked for seventy years. One begs the evicting sheriff to understand his love of the land, to let him stay. But the sheriff says he can't help because his orders came from the new administrator in Omaha, and the administrator can't help because he takes orders from the owner in San Francisco, who can't help either because he takes orders from his banker in New York. I might have blown some details but I'm sure you get the gist.

Our entire system of ownership, not just of land but also of businesses and corporations, has become about as absurd as the above movie scene. Almost no one who has final responsibility is ever anywhere near the place the damage is being done, whether environmental or social. Popular literature and films abound in the suffering caused by absentee landlords, who, as a denouement, come face to face with their sins, realize the pain they've caused and set things right again. Except that in real life the landlord seldom if ever comes.

So the planet is, bit by bit, being massacred and poisoned by absentee landlords who dump millions of gallons of herbicides and pesticides on their lands, but at their distant homes set ant traps because they don't want to poison their own gardens. Absentee owners, often innocent shareholders who invest through ever-changing portfolios so they have no idea whether they own nuclear weapons or socks, kill thousands with coal dust, asbestos, or chemical clouds, while at home in their tidy suburb they wear "Save the Planet" buttons and separate their trash.

I don't think we need a long list of examples or details. It seems only too obvious that if those who *make* the real decisions had to physically *live* with them and thus suffer the consequences, disasters like Bhopal or Love Canal would never happen, and we would be living in a much safer world; just as, if all generals and presidents were forced to be in the front lines of battles, we would have a hell of a lot fewer, and much shorter, wars.

Besides the environmental damage caused by absentee owners, there is obvious social hurt as well. It is suffered by a society of workers who lead a life of insecurity and dread, awaiting the moment when the arbitrary axe will fall and their jobs end to satisfy the profit needs or tax needs of some unknown and uninvolved owners far away. Who would argue that, if a personal bond of whatever strength existed between employer and employee, the concern for each other would be greater, and the loyalty, the sharing of problems, and the working toward common goals would be greatly enhanced?

To create a world physically healthier and socially more secure, limiting ownership to two simple practices would do. Neither of them is new; both have been used worldwide for centuries with good results. One is the employee-only-owned company; the other, the live-on-the-premises family business.

The Employee-Only-Owned Company

W.W. Norton & Company, on New York's Fifth Avenue across from the stately public library, is one of America's most respected publishers. The firm was founded by Mr. and Mrs. Norton in 1923. After her husband's death in 1945, Mrs. Norton, choosing not to sell the company to outsiders, agreed to sell her stock to the senior employees regardless of how long it might take for them to pay. To assure stability and security, an agreement was drawn up among the shareholders restricting stock ownership only to *active* employees. Those retiring or leaving for any other reason have to sell their shares back. So when Norton has a stockholders' meeting, most of the employees attend, and every attendee is an active employee.

The results have been remarkable. Not only are job security and employee attitudes infinitely better than at other publishers, but the quality of the books produced is consistently high. Norton is a medium-size company, but it has become renowned for the subject matter and authoritativeness of its books, as exemplified by *The*

Norton Anthology of English Literature. There are, of course, publishing houses with traditional forms of ownership that have gained similar status, but not in such a congenial and unpressured atmosphere. This opinion is shared by many who have come from other major publishers, and have found the ambiance of Norton like going home to Mom. I am not exaggerating when I say the staff feel and behave like a family.

Because there is so little pressure, so little backstabbing, politicking, jockeying for power or for extra paper clips—the officers get no company cars, the offices are tiny, assistants are shared, the furniture is unpretentious hand-me-downs; more time and energy can be spent in creative and productive ways. And because almost everyone has a share in the company, the pride that goes into the work is the kind one normally finds only with craftsmen working for themselves. So people stay. A receptionist just retired after thirty-seven years, an editor just completed his fortieth, and the current president his thirtieth. Since 1923 there have been only four presidents and three treasurers. The general books sales staff has been there for an average of ten years. At Norton, if you have been on the staff less than that, you are considered a newcomer.

It is the kind of place where you have only to ask for help, and you get it. When the head of a division was about to be married to someone whose work was based in Chicago, she went to the president to tell him regretfully that she had to leave. His response was, "*You* are the division. Take it with you." She did. Another employee moved her one-woman show to Denver. When an assistant began to have family problems that affected her to the point where she needed lengthy time off, Norton told her she could come back whenever she was ready. When she didn't work out as assistant to one person, others took her on. And when Norton people feel stifled in their jobs, the company tries to find them something more challenging to do. Events like these help create an atmosphere of security that is the antithesis of most other publishing houses, where it is not unheard of to go home happy on Friday only to come back on Monday to a cleaned-out desk and a two weeks' severance check.

The fact that there is no outside-ownership pressure for megaprofits, or flashy titles, has allowed Norton to be run by editors instead of by money-men. In the daily workings of the company, this translates into books that are judged by measures other than just profitability. Because of this, and because of the absence of the threat of dismissal and of the pressure to out-perform others, editors often publish their convictions—what they feel to be vital in humanitarian, intellectual or artistic terms. Hence the Norton list is noticeably short on flashy books, perhaps to the detriment of short-term balloon profits, but to the enhancement of long-term integrity, which translates into profit of a more lasting kind. None of this is written in policy papers. There are none at Norton; things seem to diffuse by osmosis. And just what constitutes a Norton book no one can say, but everyone seems to know.

How profitable the house is, is kept confidential, but it has continued through half a century with no upheavals or disasters, no great mergers, reorganizations or vicious cost-cutting, and has yielded a good living for everyone involved. Along with the money, Norton gave those who worked there an indelible, and justifiable, sense of pride, and a sense that, throughout the years, they were cared for; they belonged. And in a society driven almost exclusively by the rush for profit, a society where humanity is an expendable cost, to be cared for, to belong, is perhaps the most cherished reimbursement of all.

There have been studies done on Spanish worker-owned cooperatives that showed them to be 7.5 percent more efficient than larger enterprises, and 40 percent more efficient than medium and small ones. In his book *Good Money*, Ritchie P. Lowry cites a 1988 study that attributed their financial success to the "spirit of cooperation throughout the cooperative in contrast with the spirit of domination that often characterizes more traditional business firms."

The Live-on-the-Premises Family Business

When we escaped from Hungary to Austria in 1956 we spent the first week in a refugee camp. We had six dollars. One day a well-dressed gentleman came in and said he needed one experienced textile-dyer. The nineteen-year-old street kid we had befriended at the border immediately raised his hand. That he had worked only as a tree mover didn't give him pause. The gentleman said he would like to take him to Vienna to meet the factory owner. The street kid asked if he could take me along because I was his brother.

Both he and my parents ended up working at the textile-dyeing factory owned by the Family Edlinger. The factory was at the end of the street adjoining the Danube marshlands. From the street it looked like the other brick apartment buildings, but inside was the plant.

Beside it, facing the river, were apartments for the employees. Across from the gate, facing the street, were the apartments of the entire Edlinger family. When we arrived, they all came out to greet us.

The place was spotless. Trees and flowers everywhere, the plant clean, no fumes, no smells, no intrusive noises. The workers who lived in the apartment building were friends. They played soccer on a half-frozen field together, they ice-fished together, their kids set fire to the dead Danube reeds together, and, although I didn't see this because it was winter, they worked little vegetable gardens together across the street. I was too young to note social interaction but I do remember people speaking with pride about where they lived and worked, and an atmosphere of general good spirits everywhere, in contrast to the gloom and sniping I have seen in many plants since.

The Edlinger plant is not much different from North American company towns, but the big difference was that the owners lived and worked as close to the plant as any employee, breathed the same air, suffered the same noise, and saw working and living conditions with their own eyes every day. And that I think makes all the difference in the world.

Apart from the fact that such owner-operated and owner-and-employee-inhabited enterprises would be much less damaging both to the environment and to our social structures because both employer and employee would care more about the fallout of their actions, a most obvious bonus would be gained with the later: There would be no commuting. This not only saves staggering quantities of gasoline pollution and manufacture pollution (from the cars and buses that are not used, hence not built) but allows much stronger social bonds by allowing every family, every friend, another two hours a day to be together instead of locked into a lonely, anonymous commute.

Some may argue that to impose these limitations on free enterprise would be a violent act. There are three responses to this. First, American enterprise is nowhere near free; it is controlled by a million laws from social to environmental, all of which require millions of manhours to write, enforce, and above all, to avoid. In contrast to this, having to live with the damage and pain you cause would, without doubt, set up self-policing, self-enforcement. Second, both of the above ownerships have been tried before without trauma to anyone. In the case of employee ownership, many faltering companies like Avis and United Airlines have been saved when employees took them over. Their example is not widely followed because it was never emphasized or encouraged. And third, the discomfort caused could be no worse than what we have now—being condemned to a slow death on a dying planet.

The skeptics can laugh and say, "How can you convert giant, many-armed corporations like Dow or General Motors into the small companies your two plans would require?" Simple. You break them up. It was done to Ma Bell. Few will argue that gigantism in itself has brought any benefit to anyone except for the very few at the top who have made fortunes. In a reasonable world much of what most big corporations produce would not be needed anyway, at least certainly not in present quantities, so scaling down would by and large take care of itself.

The U-Shaped Smokestack Law

A third simple solution, not one of ownership but of husbandry, would overnight turn the world into a cleaner, safer place. This could be called the U-Shaped Smokestack Law, meaning that all the poisons produced would have to remain right where they were made. This of course would make little difference if company owner-ships were left as they are today, for the absentee owners would simply dump the poisons on the heads of their own employees instead of on the guys next door, as they are doing now. But if the smokestack law were coupled with the ownerships proposed above, and those swallow-ing the profits would also swallow the death, you can bet your life there would be a lot of redesigning and rethink-ing in a hurry. While we are putting a bend in smoke-stacks, let us also do it with sewer pipes and roads that now send poisons off to the far corners of the world.

There are a few closed-circuit plants now in existence, predominantly in Scandinavia, whose example could be followed, but it is inarguable that many of our plants would simply have to close. So much the better. A conti-nent that produces over *600 billion pounds of hazardous waste a year* could do with a few plant closings. As to what would happen to the many who would lose their jobs, well, as a just-laid-off employee of a large plant put it, "We'll just have to go back to working the family farm." There are worse things. At least farm air is clean, and the food is clean, and you can produce apples instead of poison air, and carrots instead of toxic waste. You can live and work without feeling ashamed.

8

OUR DEVASTATED AGRICULTURE

I get about $12 wholesale for every hundred pounds of milk my cows produce. Now you go over to the local high school, and the kids pay forty-five cents for one of those little lunch cartons of milk. That works out to $90 a hundred pounds. How can anybody explain it? Stop that kind of madness and America will be back on track.
——Dorothea White, 75 years old,
Dairy farmer, New Castle, Indiana

The government just won't let you alone. The government can't farm. What does it know? But by gosh it keeps trying, and meddling, and I fear it's going to be the end of us.
——Jerry Yanos, Farmer, Staughn, Indiana

The total number of farms, which are defined as places
with actual or potential sales of agricultural products of
$1,000 or more, declined from 5.9 million in 1945 to 2.2
million in 1985. . . . During that same time 7.5 million
farm jobs were lost.
—U.S. Department of Agriculture

Between 1947 and 1982 pesticide and herbicide use on
U.S. farms increased sixteenfold.
—The National Research Council

We allow the chemical death rain to fall on us as though
there were no alternative.
— Rachel Carson

By working with nature man can be prosperous, even
rich, and happy and healthy. Fighting or cheating her,
man is always defeated, poverty-stricken, bitter and mis-
erable, and eventually is destroyed himself.
—Louis Bromfield

Food is man's first need. Since ancient times much of our
lives have been spent hunting and gathering it, or, since
about 6000 years ago starting in Mesopotamia, farming
it. In North America as recently as 1900 almost 80 percent
of us lived and worked in rural areas, with nearly everyone doing work related to the land. In this century,
although we have been mechanizing and industrializing
at an unprecedented rate, the Second World War still saw
one out of four of us living on farms and close to 20
percent of the entire labor force involved in farming. By
1985 that had fallen to only 2 percent. (Which imme-

diately leads one to ask that, if only 2 percent of us are busy fulfilling our most important need, then just what the hell exactly are the other 98 percent of us busy doing?)

What we have done to our farms and farmers, both socially and environmentally, since the Second World War, is perhaps the best example of how ludicrous and malignant our world has become. Before the forties many of our farms resembled farms of old. They were usually a blend of livestock, poultry and various crops from grains to fruits. The high density animal confinement of feedlots and poultry farms was rare, and the mammoth sardine cans where thousands of beasts jostle, steam and ferment cheek to cheek were unheard of. So was the term 'Agribusiness.'

Most farmers produced forage and feed grains for their animals using ancient, natural systems of rotating crops, and returned the animal manure to the soil to fertilize it. Little if any chemical fertilizer was used. Pests were kept under control by having a greater variety of crops in smaller fields (thus avoiding the creation of veritable paradises for a single species of pest), by crop rotation (to interrupt pest food supply), by more intensive tilling and plowing, and by a "variety of cultural and biological means," involving everything from putting birdhouses in orchards to attract the birds that munch unwanted guests, to physically bringing in natural enemies like the pretty but voracious aphid-eating ladybugs, and Albert Koebele's Australian vedalia beetles, which in 1888 saved the California citrus industry from destruction. And before the forties herbicides were virtually unused. People still believed in the hoe and the plow, instead of chemical warfare.

Before the war many farms were still simply farms; that is, families owned them, lived on them, worked them with or without outside help, and sold relatively directly from them. As John Fraser Hart, the former president of The Association of American Geographers, said about the classic American farm, "Farming was a way of life rather than a business. Farmers were content to produce enough to feed and clothe their families . . . grew crops, fattened and butchered their own cattle and hogs, milked a few cows, kept a flock of chickens for eggs and Sunday dinner, tended a garden and orchard, and preserved their own fruit and vegetables for winter." And he went on to describe some of the last holdout farms in the Smoky Mountains that once typified an era.

"Wear Cove remained unspoiled in 1959. Real people still lived there, and they were living much as their fore-bears had lived for a century or more. Their farms were small, only forty acres or so. They fed themselves from tiny truck patches of sweet corn, beans, pumpkins, and squash, and preserved for the winter what they did not eat fresh. They grew field corn for the animals and tobacco as a cash crop, but the thin limestone soil had to be used with care, and much of the land was in pasture for dairy cows and beef cattle. Most farmers had a small shed for work mules and hay storage, a smokehouse where they cured the meat they had butchered, and a springhouse where they sheltered the spring where they got their drinking water. Crocks placed in the cool water were the refrigerators where fresh food was kept."

But that kind of American family farm has all but vanished. "It has had to become the family business; farmers who used to think in hundreds must now think in thousands. They have had to specialize . . . and have eliminated their less profitable activities . . . Ulcers have replaced blisters as their principal occupational complaint."

And an ever greater percentage of the land that fulfills man's first need is now owned by absentee corporations, giants that market their own processed foods, from Dole fruit juices to wine to fast-food burgers. And these faceless giants, with minuscule respect for the living land, care little about how it is worked and nurtured, as long as it renders quarterly profits. And they, with the help of endless, often devastating federal programs, have literally poisoned the land (and much of the groundwater beneath it), driven almost 8 million humans from it, replacing them with chemicals and machines, and turned the vital, closeknit, healthy rural society that for centuries stood as the very foundation of this continent, into a gutted, nationwide ghost town. With farms and machines having grown so large the countryside now seems devoid of life.

By taking a drive in the country, anyone can experience firsthand the strange mutation that has befallen the family farm. We saw our first one more than a decade ago. Candace was flying in the Canadian Soaring Championships near the foothills of the Rockies. Near the last day of the contest, the course was 150 miles into the boonies and back again. The day calmed in late afternoon, the thermals died, and Candace radioed back that she would have to land out. She circled the house of a giant farm and landed the plane in a field nearby, hoping she might at least get a good farm meal for her troubles. The family came out to greet the lady from the sky and gave her a tour. The house stood alone in the middle of 1,200 acres of soybeans. As she looked around, searching for all those things she remembered of farms, she found none: no stables, no cows, no chicken coops, no chickens, no orchards, no fruit trees—or trees of any kind—, no vegetable gardens, and strangest of all, no smells, except of the mountain of chemicals piled against the barn. In it was a two-story-tall combine with enclosed cab, AC, and stereo, driven from so high that a farmer would have as much sense of the soil as the captain of a supertanker would have of the sea. Then they invited her inside to share their Sunday dinner, which consisted of wieners boiled in their plastic envelopes, instant mashed potatoes, and mushy, pale, canned beans. And a Swanson's frozen pie for dessert. By the time I arrived, they were all staring silently at the tube.

Not so long ago the farmer and his wife were the most diverse and inventive people that walked the planet. They had to "know more about more things than anyone in another profession." The farmer had to be a botanist, biologist, carpenter, mechanic, veterinarian and midwife, weather-forecaster, and a tireless digger of the soil. The farm wife was, as often as not, a horticulturist, animal handler, culinary wizard, food-preserving expert, accountant, and confessor, who sat with endless patience and heard her husband's woes. And they both had to have the calm of a philosopher and the patience of a saint to survive all the adversities man and God heaped on them. Almost as important, they had to be first class human beings and even better friends, for on farms of old everyone needed the help of his neighbor to survive. And most farmers were all that and more. As Louis Bromfeld wrote in the late 1930s, "For companionship, good conversation, intelligence and the power of stimulating one's mind, there are none I would place above a good farmer."

The family staring at the tube was none of the above. They drove a tractor and drove a combine and that's all. They might as well have been driving a shuttle bus in Disneyland.

This is not to say anything against the family. They did what they had to. As Terry Francl of the American Farm Bureau said, "On a typical midwestern crop farm today, you're going to need 600 to 700 acres to make enough money to support a family." And when you're struggling with 700 acres, paying the mortgage on the land, on the machines, and even on the seeds you plant, you have to specialize, and produce. You can't afford the time to become versatile or patient, or even to grow nutritious, healthy food to feed yourself. It is cheaper and faster to buy wieners at the store.

And the farms are getting bigger every year. It is the law of the market. As a farmer retires, his land is not bought up by some poor young upstart with a passion for the soil, but by a big-farmed neighbor with a big line of credit who can offer more. And as the population of the countryside dies out, so do the small towns that for years supplied the farms. Some experts say that for every six farmers that leave the land, "a business on Main Street has to close its doors." As an example, 5 percent of the population of Iowa moved away from the state in the 80s, leaving half-deserted towns in their wake. And things are not about to change. A 1990 Congressional Budget Office report foresaw that "maintaining the 1988 level of average farm net income would require that nearly a half-a-million farms leave the sector within the next five years."

So the old tightly-knit society of congenial farmer neighbors who helped each other without asking when the need arose, whether it was raising a barn or curing a sick cow, is becoming, bit by bit, a society of distant strangers. "We don't really know the neighbors," Orris Rogers, an Iowa corn farmer, said. "If I broke my leg nobody around here would even know about it." And this antisocial character of the new rural North America drives almost as many of the young would-be farmers from the land as do the economic demands involved in starting up a farm—estimated by some to be $200,000. So the Future Farmers of America Club has lost more than 20 percent of its members since 1980, and half of those left said they won't be farming. When the people are gone and the opportunities are gone there is not much left to stay for.

And as great as the social destruction is, the environmental and health damage is even greater. As each man leaves, he is replaced by chemicals and still bigger machines that bode worse times for the future. Already farming is the greatest non-point (not from an easily locatable point like a factory) polluter of surface water on the continent with the chemical residue from fertilizers, pesticides, and herbicides. In addition to that is the pollution from their production and application with tractors, helicopters, and planes. Now imagine what will happen if another half-million farmers and their families—but not their cultivated fields—disappear. The big new machines damage the very soil. The more their power and speed increase, the more topsoil they throw into the air to be blown away. Just watch the great dust cloud that follows giant tractors.

Now many say that lamenting the passing of the family farm is all romantic bunk, that the world is simply unfolding as it must, and anyway, small farmers are as likely to use chemicals and destroy the soil as big ones. But this just isn't true. In our valley in Tuscany, the contrasts still live side by side. Along our road, four families out of five still make their living working family farms, none of them bigger than forty acres and two of them less than twenty. Beyond our house are the vast vineyards of a corporation from Rome.

By the end of May, the vines are full of leaves and tiny clusters of young grapes. In Paolucci's small vineyard, the end of May will have seen him pass but once with his small tractor and plow, to bury the weeds and to let the rains of June penetrate the soil, and return later with a small sprayer to spray the leaves with fungicide. In the vineyards of the corporation, the first tractor comes in April as soon as the buds have greened, roaring between the rows of vines, spewing, with huge rotor-fans, clouds of fungicides. They come three times in May—once to disc the ground, once to spray herbicide, and then once with the fungicide. So there you have the difference. In five weeks the small farmer made one pass with a plow and one with a controlled spray, while the corporation made four, three of which spewed chemicals of who-knows-how-strong venom.

You may think I am overreacting in using the word venom, but that just isn't so. Pesticides, herbicides and fungicides are created for one reason only—to kill living organisms. The "cide" ending on these words comes from the Latin meaning "kill," and is used with no less malice or fatality than in homi*cide.*

The absurdity of using all this venom to grow our food is almost beyond comment. As writer/organic grower Eliot Coleman so understatedly put it, "The idea of striving to create lifegiving and nourishing food crops while simultaneously dousing them with deadly poisons seems inherently contradictory."

The United States alone uses 500 million pounds of pesticides a year, of which it is estimated as little as 0.1 percent actually reaches its intended victims, while the rest ends up in our water, soil and food. According to the Worldwatch Institute, through "routine agricultural practices, groundwater has been contaminated with more than fifty different pesticides in at least thirty states. . . . More than a quarter of Iowans use drinking water contaminated with pesticides."

Our fruits, vegetables and even meats—animals eat the poisoned feed and store them in their tissues in highly concentrated form—are so dense in pesticidal residue that they were found to be of "serious concern" in a 1987 study by the National Research Council. As reported by Worldwatch, "In its worst-case estimate, the study calculated an increased risk of 5,800 cancer cases per million people over a 70-year lifetime, far higher than the 1 per million 'acceptable' risk level that the Environmental Protection Agency often applies to cancer hazards. This translates to roughly 1.4 million additional cancer cases for the current U.S. population. . . . Nearly 80 percent of the estimated risk is derived from just fifteen foods, with tomatoes, beef, potatoes, oranges and lettuce leading the list."

So, the next time you order an old-fashioned chicken sandwich with a side of fries and a salad, do what Jack Nicholson did in *Five Easy Pieces*; tell the waitress to hold the chicken, potatoes, tomatoes and lettuce and just bring you bread. And one last suggestion—while you are awaiting your meal, *don't drink the water!*

The most shocking thing of all is that we continue to poison ourselves while an infinite variety of safe methods exist. Don't forget that all of this "death rain " didn't start falling until after the Second World War. Humanity had eaten perfectly well before and has developed many new ways to eat safely since. So why this sudden chemical warfare against ourselves? As Rachel Carson wrote, "Future historians may well be amazed at our distorted sense of proportion. How could intelligent beings seek to control a few unwanted species by a method that contaminated the entire environment and brought the threat of disease and death even to their own kind?"

And by what right do a few in power decide that it is perfectly acceptable to slowly poison millions who have little knowledge of and even less control over what we are fed?! Again Rachel Carson, "If the Bill of Rights contains no guarantee that a citizen shall be secure against lethal poisons distributed either by private individuals or public officials, it is surely only because our forefathers, despite their considerable wisdom and foresight, could conceive of no such problem."

And the irony is that we are getting nowhere. Insects, weeds and fungi have simply mutated and developed immunities, "mechanisms for detoxifying and resisting the action of chemicals designed to kill them." For example: before World War II, science had recorded only seven species of insects and mites that had developed pesticide resistance. By the mid-eighties there were 447, including all of the most devastating pests. Or take weeds. Before 1970 weed resistance was almost unheard of. Today there are forty-eight poison-resistant species.

At this point many will insist that government holds a tight rein on such things, tests things, controls things, protects us from harm. But even an ostrich knows better than that. Remember Love Canal? Thalidomide? Asbestos? Silicone implants? And remember S&L? Of course there exist a million laws; tolerances (levels of acceptability), directions of use, etc., but most of these are not only impossible to enforce (it is estimated that more than 90 percent of our foods escape inspection; see "Canadian Meat" later) but also are meaningless and even laughable in the way they are thought up.

As an example: There are over 700 pesticides and other chemicals in use on farms today. These have all been tested for cancer-causing characteristics, and acceptable levels in our food were established for them. That is to say, it was *estimated* that, when ingested by humans, x-quantity of product y would have "no more than one-in-a-million chance" of causing cancer.

But how they were tested and approved is another matter. First, many of them are old products, and "current federal pesticide regulatory policy applies a stricter standard to new pesticides . . . than to older pesticides approved before 1972." This in spite of the fact that a small number of older pesticides seem to present "the vast majority of health and environmental risks associated with pesticides." Second, most of the products were tested by the manufacturers themselves and the data then presented to the government for evaluation. This is much like asking a goat to count the heads of lettuce. After all, remember how Dow Chemical's own damaging reports on the dangers of silicone implants were suppressed for years. And how the cigarette industry's own thirty-year-old study, which warned that their products are carcinogenic, was only recently brought to light.

And third, and *most important*, all the pesticides were tested individually. That is to say they were found to cause cancer one in a million times *when ingested alone*. But

we never ingest one chemical alone. We ingest an uncountable variety of them every day. As Dr. Epstein of
the Department of the Environment at the University of
Illinois in Chicago said, "One apple alone may contain
many carcinogens, and a whole plate of food, hundreds of
thousands." And what about a smorgasbord? Or as
Rachel Carson wrote, "It is quite possible that no one of
these exposures alone would be sufficient to precipitate
malignancy—yet any single supposedly 'safe dose' may
be enough to tip the scales that are already loaded with
other 'safe doses'."

So then, what *combined* effect all these modern condi-
ments may have, no one knows. No one has ever tested—
it would be almost impossible—and no one can guess.
And even if all the tests were negative, and even if only the
specified amount of residue was left in or on a vegetable or
fruit, we would be safe in eating it, who is going to
inspect the billion pounds of food we eat every day? Food
inspectors? How many hundred thousands of them? And
what political limitations do they work under and with
what results?

Last fall the *New York Times* ran an article titled, "Poisoned Meat from Canada," and subtitled it, "U.S. inspec-
tions are dangerous to your health." The article's poisoned meat was not smuggled in, but was let through by
law. The Agriculture Department's new streamlining
policy inspects only one out of fifteen trucks. But it is how
the inspection of that one truck is done that's enough to
give you a fright. When a slaughterhouse has a truckload
of meat to go, it calls the Agriculture Department,
"which uses a random-sampling computer program to
determine whether the shipment will be inspected and, if
so, whether the meat will be given a visual testing or a

laboratory test, or both. The slaughterhouse is notified *before the truck leaves. It* segregates the chosen samples from the rest of the shipment for inspection; they are wrapped in plastic and put inside the truck's rear doors. If inspectors enter trucks and choose their own samples, they are subject to reprimand or dismissal." If that doesn't sound like something from Kafka, I don't know what does.

But even with the samples carefully chosen in advance, one inspector, William J. Lehman of Montana, says he rejects from "40 to 80 percent of the meat" because of "pus-filled abscesses, sticky layers of bacteria leaving a stench, fecal contamination stains . . . and metal shavings." Consumers can apparently contract food poisoning from contaminated meat. (I'm not sure what they get from metal shavings besides Roto-rootering their intestines.) The symptoms can take up to twenty-four hours to manifest themselves; besides, they resemble those of the flu, so most people never even guess what they might have had.

So there you have government inspection in a nutshell. And if something as obvious as "stenchy" meat gets by, what snowball's chance in hell do we have against pesticide residues that are judged safe at one part per billion but dangerous at two?

Then there are the reversals of certain government decisions, according to who in power is how much in debt to whom, that truly boggle the mind and scare other body parts into movement. The *New York Times* reported such a one in February of 1992. There was a family of pesticides developed in the late 1940s to protect against a fungus that sometimes destroyed crops and sometimes ruined their looks. (I mean who wants to eat a homely piece of broccoli?!) Then in 1987, within a political blink of an eye, the National Academy of Sciences identified the chemicals—mancozeb, maned, and metiram—as "among the most potent carcinogens used in agriculture." (All those who ate pretty broccoli in the last forty years, start sweating.) The manufacturers of the chemicals realized this was not the greatest news, so they voluntarily agreed to end use of the chemicals on all but thirteen crops while *they*—the manufacturers—awaited the results of tests *they* were conducting in cities around the country to measure how much residue remained on food. (So now we have the rabbits counting carrots.) In late 1991 the findings were released, and—you'll never guess—the "most potent carcinogens" were suddenly no problem. William K. Reilly, the E.P.A. administrator gushed about how "good science" did its job providing better data and suggestions on how farmers can apply the chemicals so as not to leave enough venom to kill us one and all. Something about using eyebrow pencils. But one of the big achievements of "good science" was to determine that it is silly to measure residue on produce at the farm (where presumably only the farmer and his friends and neighbors eat it). Instead it should be measured at the supermarket where most of us shop anyway. "Good science" concluded that by the time the food got to the supermarket, such a long period of time had passed that the venom had decomposed and had become as benign as powdered sugar. In other words: The last thing you want to do is eat your fresh fruits and vegetables *fresh*. Always ask for the oldest, half-rotten ones; they're the safest.

So anyway, the ban was lifted and farmers now spray away. But there is one twist. The most potent carcinogen is powdered sugar only on "apples, barley, broccoli, cabbage, lettuce, cucumber, eggplant, and twenty-two other crops." It is still considered a potent carcinogen when used on "apricot, celery, peaches and spinach." Get it?! Of course not. You see, *this* is why it is best to leave these things to the government because dumb-dumbs like you and I just don't understand.

The most disgusting thing about this "rain of death" is that it need never have happened. It came about because of pressure on government *by the big chemical companies* to promote toxins. This chemical warfare against ourselves was then organized and aided by disastrous federal laws, in the form of tax incentives, subsidies, commodity programs, and deficiency payments, which often can be "a substantial portion of a farmer's gross income," and often all of his profit. Hence, farmers often joke about "farming the government," for they do not adjust their crops to either the biological and physical needs of their particular lands or even to the markets, but rather to the current government programs that yield the most.

A National Research Council study summed up the effect of subsidies this way: "Fertilizers and pesticides are often applied at rates that cannot be justified economically without consideration of farm program payments. Federal programs . . . encourage unrealistically high yield goals, inefficient pesticide and fertilizer use, and unsustainable use of land and water." This is done in three ways. One, pesticides and fertilizers are "poured on" to increase yields on good land and maximize government program payments. Two, even worse pouring on occurs as farmers "expand crop production onto marginal lands . . . or regions poorly suited to a particular crop," to cash in on the giveaway. And three, subsidies promote specialization in one or two crops, and continuous planting (instead of crop rotation), thereby creating the paradise for pests, which, in turn, will require vastly increased use of pesticides.

The report comes to this overall conclusion: "Federal policy has no coherent strategy or national goals to unite the programs, nor is there much appreciation of what the programs do or should accomplish or how they interact." To put it in plain English: No one knows diddly-squat! The report goes on: "This 'crises-oriented policy-making' only reacts; it doesn't anticipate. In more than half a century of operation, government policy has not only affected prices and output, but has also shaped technological change, encouraged uneconomical investment in machinery and facilities, inflated the value of the land, subsidized crop production practices that have led to soil, surface and groundwater pollution . . . and contributed to the demise of the railway systems. . . . Government policy has had a far-reaching influence on agriculture, much of it unintended and unanticipated." Put *that* on our tombstones.

The irony of all this is that all the while there are highly profitable alternative farming systems in operation, that use, among other things, crop rotation to disrupt the reproductive cycle and food supply of pests, "less synthetic chemical pesticides, fertilizers and antibiotics *per unit of production* than comparable conventional farms, without decreasing and in some cases increasing per-acre crop yields and the productivity of livestock." And, they "usually function with little help from subsidized programs." In other words, they do less harm to us physically and they don't eat up taxes. But the alternative farmers are the rare outsiders. Would it not make infinitely more sense for all of agriculture to begin phasing out chemicals, both fertilizers and pesticides, and embrace their system?

Critics of this idea argue that this would eliminate from use marginal lands that were made productive only "by pouring on the fertilizer" and poisons. So much the better. The worldwide problem is overproduction, so cutting back could only help. Besides, the good farmer, who has used care in selecting his soil, who chose crops to suit the soil, will not suffer. It will mostly be the thoughtless farmer who suffers, he who has tried with chemicals to squeeze blood out of the stone.

Now it is true that for a while, until we all become experts at more natural farming, some production costs might rise and so would the price of food. Well and good. A continent that spends $35 billion a year on weight reduction could stand to eat a little less. Or we can, as a last resort, learn to cook again instead of paying for processing, which makes up about 70 percent of our food bill. I know this might take some work and thinking, but then that's why God made us people and not tapeworms. And the farmers could sure use some added income. Perhaps few things are as indicative of our society of madness than that those who feed us are one step ahead of bankruptcy, while millions of public and private bureaucrats and middlemen, who do God only knows what, can barely keep up with spending the money thrown at them.

Economists may claim that allowing prices of food produced in North America to rise would simply turn over the market to cheaper imports using poisons. Well, the "new world order" could certainly include unpoisoned food for all. Alternative agriculture should be a global priority. Its flourishing would not only help reverse the environmental devastation modern farming has wreaked, but also help revitalize country life. People could, for once, replace poisons and machines. And it would help re-create a stable farm community. It would help in the rebirth of the small, self-sufficient, almost non-polluting, diverse family farm, one teeming with variety and life, where a family could live without the dreaded bank loans, where farmers could farm the soil and not the government, where they and their families could, as Louis Bromfield said, "enjoy the greatest of all gifts Nature can bring to Man—a piece of good land, with the good rich food, the independence, the security, the excitement and even splendor that goes with it."

9

TRUE SECURITY
IN THE COUNTRY

*What attracted me to Europe and most of all to France
was the sense of continuity and permanence of small but
eternal things, of the incredible resistance and resiliency of
the small people.*

*The permanence, the continuity of France was a living
thing, anchored to the soil, to the very earth itself. Any
French peasant, any working man with his little plot of
ground and his modest home and wages which by American standards were small, had more permanence, more
solidity, more security, than the American workingman
or white-collar worker who received, according to French
standards, fabulous wages, who rented (or mortgaged) the
home he lived in and was perpetually in debt for his car,
his radio, his washing machine. . . . It seemed to me
that real continuity, real love of one's country, real permanence, had to do not with mechanical inventions and high
wages but with the earth and man's love of the soil upon
which he lived.*

—Louis Bromfield

Jackson, New Hampshire

The tiny village of Jackson straddles the Wildcat River, just below Jackson Falls, in the White Mountains of New Hampshire. You approach it on curvy mountain roads. In the winter you wind among snow-draped forests and streams so thick with ice that the surging water breaks through only now and then.

On one side of the river, the bay-windowed hotel dates from 1869, the church, with its open belfry and white steeple, from 1847, and the squat library, like a fanciful old barn, from the turn of the century. Across the bridge are scattered the post office, two eateries, some shops, and the Jackson Grammar School, as pretty a New England clapboarder as you have seen.

The land in these parts is not a farmer's dream. The latitude is high, the winter long—apple trees seldom blossom before Memorial Day. The terrain is hilly and tiring, and the soil is so rocky that a tractor has to plow one furrow at a time instead of the four or five furrows it could do in decent soil. In the winter the winds are foul. Atop Mount Washington, a few miles north of town, the wind often reaches eighty miles an hour, bringing the wind-chill factor to minus 100 degrees Fahrenheit, below which no one has ever bothered to keep score. The Davis family has farmed the same piece of land here for nine generations.

They live two miles north of Jackson at the foot of Black Mountain on a sprawling farm of 320 acres. Half of it is fields and open pasture, the other half a forest of sugar maple, birch, ash, and in the higher portions, clusters of fir and pine. Bob Davis, his wife Bea and one of their three sons live in the big frame house built by his great-

great-grandfather in 1863. The great wood barn, with its foundation of dry-laid fieldstone, was put up the same year.

Forty years ago, these hills were all worked by families like the Davises, most of them with less land, all of them engaged, like the Davises, in widely mixed farming— sugaring the maple forest in the winter, growing corn, raising cattle, pigs, and poultry for meat, running dairies, and tending fields of pumpkins. As recently as the nineteen-sixties, between here and Conway, where the bottom land is more plentiful, there were twenty-five good-sized dairies, some running fifty milkers, some nearly three hundred. But the valley has changed drastically since then. The dairies have closed down and the farms have been sold off piece by piece to week-enders from distant towns who build condominiums and chalets. But Bob Davis and his family have stayed on.

Their farming now is more mixed than ever. With his two grown sons working with him, Bob Davis, now fifty-three years old, tall, gaunt, quiet, with a mind as sharp and quick and witty as you'd find anywhere, talks first about the livestock which "we feed every morning before we feed ourselves." In the winter that means mushing through snow and darkness to the barn that's warm and humid from the bodies of the cattle, cutting open fresh bales of hay and pitching them into the troughs or just in piles on the dirt floor. In the summer, the cows roam the pastures or the woods in search of exotic fodder. They raise twenty-five head at a time now, about half dairy cows that they raise from calves until they freshen—meaning they can calve—at two-and-a-half years, and the other half for meat, slaughtering, dressing, and selling them—usually by the side—to neighbors in the valley. The cattle weigh around 500 pounds when dressed, and the past years have been fetching close to $1.20 a pound or $600 a cow. A half a cow they freeze up, and that keeps them in beef for the year.

The fifty acres of hay that they cut and bail yields 8,000 bales. Of this, their own cattle eat 3,000, the rest they sell off at $1.20 a bail in the summer from the field, or $2.00 a bail in fall and winter from the barn. So the hay they sell off can bring $6,000 to $8,000 a year; nothing to jump up and down about, but it's a start. They have a hundred acres that's plain pasture, and since cattle don't need more than an acre a head, they take in cow boarders in the months the grass grows well. And they cultivate an acre of sweet corn and an acre of pumpkins, both of which they sell direct, for about $2,000 a year.

Then there are the chickens. Their numbers vary with the seasons but there are normally twenty-five being raised as roasters or fryers, which they sell at eight weeks for $4 a head. They keep about sixty layers, who lay four dozen eggs a day. The eggs are set in cardboard cartons on the kitchen table; the door is always unlocked, and people come and help themselves and leave $1.20 per dozen in a cup.

From late spring on there is the vegetable garden. It is about forty by a hundred feet, on the flat top of a hill that gets the longest hours of sun. Here Bea grows everything—peas, beans, carrots, onions, broccoli—and what they don't eat fresh she 'freezes up' and they eat it through the winter.

They also keep two pigs, one to slaughter in the spring and one in the fall, for ham, pork chops and bacon. So through the mild season the pantry builds up and the treasury builds up and, what is just as important, the spirit stays fresh because the work is always varied. There are different jobs, different seasons, in the fields, in the forest, in the barn, and, within limits, you are free to choose the chore that suits your mood. And that surely is a far cry from the redundant, choiceless drudgery most city workers are condemned to all year. This variety is a boon not only to the spirit but also to the family's security. If any single crop fails, or livestock falters, there are other things to fall back on, unlike the monocrop large-scale farmer, or monojob city dweller, whose single loss can lead to financial disaster.

In the winter the world changes on the Davis farm. The leaves are gone by late October and the cold winds from Canada begin blowing down the valley. The corn and the pumpkins have been picked and sold, and the vegetable garden is wilted and empty save for the po-tatoes huddled underground. Bob Davis and his sons head up into the woods. There are always fallen trees from last winter's storms to be cleaned and cut with chainsaws, pulled down the hill by tractor, bucked, cut up, then, without splitting, laid up for a couple of years to dry. They need eight cords for themselves for the winter but they don't stop there. Woods as large as theirs, care-fully managed, can yield a lot of firewood and have for generations. So the Davises take as much as a hundred fifty cords every winter, to lay up, while they pull out the seasoned wood, split it and deliver it in the valley for $100 a cord.

When the snow falls—nowadays much less frequently than before—they hook a snowplow on the tractor and plow the roads and driveways in the valley. Every bit helps. They don't get rich pushing snow around, but it helps them buy a better grade machine, better gear, and that can make a lot of difference on a farm.

Then there is the sugar orchard. There is a twenty-acre orchard in the hills with 1,800 good-size sugar maples in it. For generations "sugaring" was the year's highlight on the Davis farm, marking, as it always did, the end of the long winter. But the activity was not only to celebrate the approaching spring, not only to look forward to remuneration for their labor. It was one of the times of year when young and old worked together, and the valley's kids all came just for the fun of trudging through the snow with flapping snowshoes, or driving the team of horses that pulled the big wood sleigh hauling the wood tank sloshing full of sap, or spending hours by the blazing fire under the big iron evaporator in the sugar house feeding the roaring flames with three-foot hunks of wood, milling about in the great billows of steam that belched out of the shadows, bucketing in the sap and bucketing out the syrup, then 'slumping' back into the snowy woods for more.

But sugaring was no frivolous party. You slumped through the woods on snowshoes, a tiring chore even empty-handed, and you lurched from tree to tree with a pair of five-gallon tin buckets, filling them with sap. When the buckets were full and the snow soft, you sank in a good foot-and-a-half on every step, buckets, snowshoes, curses and all; then, all out of breath, you yanked your foot out and slumped on and thanked God for the horses because they came when you whistled and saved you a trip back. There was no time to waste; when the sap ran, you ran.

But when things go well sugaring is a dream and the money is good. You haul a lot of sap—thirty to forty-five gallons of it for every precious gallon of sweet syrup at the end. There was a time when the Davis family bottled up to 400 gallons of syrup in a good year, and Bob's grandmother sold it all, a small jug at a time, by mail order, all over the country. Even now, when working fewer trees brings in much less syrup, the thirty-five dollars they get for every gallon helps to keep the family kitty just a little fatter.

Besides the haying, the cattle, the chickens, corn, pumpkins, firewood, snow-shoveling and the maple syrup, Bob Davis and his sons do some house maintenance and carpentry in the summer, time permitting, and cut hay for others when the season comes. In New Hampshire, where the growing season is short, you have to be adaptable to survive.

It must be obvious by now that living off the land in northern New Hampshire is no permanent vacation. But I chose New Hampshire for just that reason, for if the Davises have managed in this changing, rocky place of long cold winters for nine generations, then one can certainly survive working the rich soils in the better climates of Virginia or Alberta or Oregon. But Bob Davis and his family have stayed because they like the silence, like the trees, like being their own bosses. The one thing that Bob Davis misses is the people, not the unknown masses that now amble every weekend through the towns, but the friends who have moved away, been forced off the land. Sometimes he thinks of moving on to a less changed place, away from tourists, back among small farmers, back to where the neighbors are still friends, like they were here forty years ago.

A Tuscan Family Farm

Perhaps a more ideal example of small-scale farming—if for no other reason than the climate is much kinder *and* most neighbors are still working the land—is that of the Paoluccis, in central Italy. Their valley is one of the most beautiful in all of Tuscany. It was once ocean bottom—with almost every shovelful you dig up a fossil—so the hills are softly rounded, gently rolling, reflecting the endless motion of the sea, the flowing of the tides, the sculpting of the currents. In early summer when the wheat is green and the winds blow hard, the hills and valleys ripple like the ocean.

The Paoluccis' house sits on a narrow clay road that runs along a ridge in the middle of the valley. When I say narrow, I mean if two cars meet, one has to back up to let the other pass. And when I say "on" the road, I mean you have to take care the hay-cart doesn't knock a cornerstone from the wall. This to us North Americans might seem a strange location for a house, for we like to be far from roads and other people to escape noise and unwanted eyes. But the Italian countryside is quiet and the neighbors constitute much of the social life. For a neighbor to pass by without stopping for a word would be almost like slapping a friend.

Anyway, the house is on the road and the Paoluccis' seven hectares—about seventeen acres—straddle it. (Oddly enough, this is about the size of cultivated land Bob Davis would start with were he to do it again.) The Paoluccis' rolling land is made up of fields of various shapes and sizes and more types of crops than you can count on both your hands. The biggest single crop is seven acres of grain, mostly wheat, rotating sometimes with oats, sometimes with alfalfa to replenish the soil. Some of the wheat is fine-milled for pasta and bread for the family, some coarse-milled for the pigs, cows, chickens, ducks and uncountable other fowl, and the rest, about five tons, is sold for about $1,500. Note how closely the activities and incomes of this Italian farm resemble those of the Davis farm in New Hampshire. After the grain fields, the next biggest are in hay to feed the cows and rabbits, then come the smaller fields, the true treasures of the farm, which yield the most valuable crops.

No one is sure how many acres the vineyard takes up because there are three *vignas* of rather bizarre shapes, but there are 1,500 grapevines altogether, yielding an annual harvest of eighty *quintales* or 17,500 pounds of grapes. About one quarter of this is made into wine for the family, some made into wine and sold direct in demi-johns or bottles, while the rest is sold fresh to large *cantinas* who buy grapes from different growers to make wine. The vineyard income varies, depending on how much is sold and how. If you sell the 13,000 pounds of grapes fresh off the vine, they bring a little over three thousand dollars. If you take the time to turn the grape to wine yourself, you can sell it *sfuso*, or bulk, for about twice the price.

Even more treasured than vineyards are olive groves. Tuscan olive oil is flavorful, pungent and sought after, and it sells for $18 a kilo; about $8 a pound, direct from the farm. No farmhouse would be thought complete without a year's supply safely in the cantina in clay jars, and few things are valued higher than your own olive orchard. Growing olives is a farmer's dream, occasional murderous frosts notwithstanding. You plow the grove but once or twice a year, spread manure from the stalls once, and while it is true that the harvesting is slow—olive by

113

olive, all by hand—an old tree can yield up to fifty kilos of oil, and at $18 a kilo that's a lot.

But the mainstays at the Paoluccis are the various animals they raise around the house. From the litters of two pigs they keep two or three piglets for themselves, the rest they raise for two to three months, then they sell them off at market for $120 each. But the most highly sought-after meat is milk-fed veal. Paolucci usually has three calves at a time in the stalls and he can normally sell them at four months for about $3 a pound. They also sell dressed chickens and rabbits to people who come from town, and the chickens lay about a dozen eggs a day, some of which get sold off, the rest kept to nourish the family.

Including the hard-currency beasts, the Paoluccis' menagerie looks normally like this: three cows, three calves, two pigs (about twenty piglets around Easter), forty chickens, two turkeys, fifteen rabbits, twenty pigeons, ten ducks, a pony, a kid, a lamb and a goat. The pony is for riding around the countryside, and everything else is grown to be eaten.

The rest of their food comes from the garden. It is spread out in three places on the farm. The hundreds of potato, onion, chickpea, bean, and tomato plants are in the lower fields away from the house, while things like parsley, radishes, zucchini, peas and artichokes, needing attention, are nearer the house where they can be watered on hot summer days.

Fruit trees are everywhere. *Susine*, a smallish local plum, grows wild here and is used for jams, preserves and baking. Peaches, pears, cherries and apricots yield small crops in the hard clay soil but their flavors are said (at least by locals) to be the envy of all Italy. What they don't eat in the summer they preserve for winter. Tomatoes are either stewed or sun-dried, artichokes are kept in oil, all fruits are canned, the pigs killed and the great prosciutto hams cured in salt and hung up in the cantina with the sausages and bacon.

As I said, the great fireplace in the kitchen heats the house in winter. Fires in the wood stove all year round make those wonderful roast ducks, roast rabbits and roast pigeons. The wood for both of these Paolucci cuts in a forest two miles up the valley, and hauls it home on a cart behind the tractor. He shares the cut wood equally with the forest's owner.

The Paoluccis' farm is as unmechanized as a modern farm can get. There is only one tractor, twenty years old, that he uses about 150 hours a year for everything from plowing to hauling hay and wood and grapes or casks of wine. They also have a small machine, for cutting hay, that looks like a kid's bike with a long, wide blade attached oddly to its side, and they have a car, a little Fiat, and an Ape, which is a three-wheeled truck that's really a 100cc motorbike with sheet metal wrapped around it and a small flatbed behind it to haul a load and keep you out of the rain. And a bicycle.

Their farm needs little from outside sources. They feed the animals only what they grow, and, in return, the animals provide manure for the crops. The Paoluccis produce almost no garbage and no waste. Their self-reliance is so profound that if the rest of the world all went to hell tomorrow, they would hardly notice. And they eat better food—fresher, more nourishing, more flavorful—than any king.

Maybe it is the smallness of the farm, or maybe it's the tiny fields of many shapes and colors with the ducks and chickens roaming the fields and gardens, and the pigeons swooping loudly overhead, and a pig sleeping here, a cow tethered there, with the haystacks neatly lined up near the house, the wood stacked, the fruit trees pruned, the lake shimmering and the smoke always curling from the chimney, but the old stone house and its surroundings look as much like a fairy tale setting as you would let yourself believe.

It is true the hours are long. The day starts at six-thirty with the feeding of the animals, and ends around six in summer and about four in winter—with those memorable five-course lunches in between. But what never seems to change at the Paoluccis, regardless of the season, what has always seemed remarkable to me, is the pace. Franco never hurries. When I help him with the hay, or the *vendemmia*, or the olives, the phrase I most often hear is "*Piano—piano*", which means, "Slowly—slowly."

This is a sign of neither laziness nor a lack of strength. The man has muscles like rocks and works every day but Sunday. But there exists an inimitable leisure in his life; something calm, something tranquil, a kind of peace, as if he always were—which he always is—at home. And I'm not talking about some pious holy man, but a devout Italian who will roar at the top of his lungs in the house or in the fields, who will laugh uproariously or howl in blazing fury; but around this boisterous life, or more correctly, under it, is a serene lake of contentment—the joy of being alive. He is unhurried because each moment is good; he doesn't need to rush to get to something better.

So Paolucci lives and works *piano . . . piano*. He gathers clover for the rabbits and stops for a chat, or to watch the birds, or walks down to the pond to see the ducks or sits for a while on his worn stone steps and tilts the two-liter bottle of wine that's always there, and pours himself a glass . . . *piano*.

But to pretend that farmwork is all strolling around the fields picking daisies would be sheer fantasy. Franco's wife has shoulders broader than mine, and Nonna, who turned 80 last year, has strength from a life of labor that lets her throw a bale of hay up on the cart with me still hooked onto it; and Paolucci's hands are gnarled and craggy from the dry clay sucking at them. To pretend that the farm is heaven would be leaving out shoveling pig shit and cow shit, and sitting on the open tractor in the blazing sun, and loading those cursed bales of hay in sizzling July. It would be to leave out the fear of drought year after year, the fear of rain, the worry about animal health, insects, molds and foxes. But, rising every morning on a farm instead of in an artificial suburb or a cell of an apartment, and seeing the sun rise over hills and trees instead of behind smokestacks; walking to the barn on a silent dusty road sparkling with dew instead of driving bumper to bumper on some endless freeway; smelling the fresh dawn and the live barn instead of smog and fumes; looking up and seeing sky instead of ceiling tiles; spending the day roaming the hills under the sun filling your lungs with clean air with every breath instead of being shut in a box breathing reconstituted air; compared to that half-life in the city, shoveling pig shit is truly paradise.

10

UNLIVABLE CITIES

The population of the West is now 86 percent urbanized. The Northeast 79 percent. California 93 percent.
—United States Census Bureau 1991

There is nothing for us to do around here but crime.
—Sincere Ailas, 17

In the United States between 1960 and 1990 the number of violent crimes per capita grew by 355 percent.
—FBI statistics

Los Angeles discharges 125 million pounds of hazardous pollutants onto itself each year. About 10 percent of them are known to be cancer-causing.
—The EPA and *The Nation*

*"Under the influence of cultural urges, some civiliza-
tions . . . , possibly the whole of mankind, have become
neurotic."* —Freud

Our big cities are sick. New York City alone has ninety
thousand homeless and one million on welfare; parts of
Los Angeles look like they have just lost a war; the spread
of AIDS and the resurgence of TB, both "inseparable
from poverty," have even the most rational among us
terrified; crime has turned whole neighborhoods into war
zones, and even in safe areas we now live behind dead-
bolts, alarms, electronic and human surveillance, and,
instead of pink flamingos, we decorate our front lawns
with signs reading "Armed Response." Our public institutions, once a main justification for embracing city life,
are undergoing quiet devastation; schools, libraries and
hospitals, already woefully inadequate, are cutting back.

We all have a favorite scapegoat to blame for the collapse of our cities: the long recession, inept or corrupt
politicians, the "lazy" poor whose welfare needs are
draining off precious funds, the "vicious" rich who are
not donating any, or the "alienated" middle class who
don't give a damn. Some even close eyes and minds and
blame it all on drugs. But kneejerk blaming will solve
nothing. We have to rout out the problems at the source.
As the commander of the New York Police Department's
narcotics division, Francis C. Hall, remarked while looking at two tons of recently seized cocaine, "You have to
ask yourself—'Why is it there are so many people in this
country who want drugs?' That is the issue that has to be
addressed. *'Why?'*"

And while we are probing the fundamental issue in the
drug scourge, we would do well to probe our whole

society and ask, "Why are our politicians so corrupt, our poor so needy, our middle class so alienated, our rich so vicious?" This kind of in-depth probing will go against our grain, for we are, above all, a quick-fix culture; sharp at handling emergencies but too dumb to avoid them. The best example might be our war on cancer. We have concentrated on curing the very sick and diagnosing the suspect. This twin approach led the National Cancer Institute in 1982 to set a goal of "reducing cancer deaths by 50 percent by the end of the century." Yet the mortality rate today is actually *higher*. We are now, finally, beginning to suspect that the only way to get cancer under control is by naming and eliminating its *causes*. And more and more its causes seem to be the environment in which we live; what we come in contact with, what we breathe, what we ingest.

Our cities may be no different. Just as our devastating physical diseases are often caused by our lifestyle—where and how we live—, so might our social ills. Just as the horrors of modern life can, through microscopic particles, electronic fields and radiation, form physical tumors in our bodies, so may our enormous social horrors, our dehumanized cities, form emotional tumors in our souls. Are not most of Freud's "cultural urges" that may have caused "the whole of mankind (to) have become neurotic," being constantly emitted—like some social radiation—from colossal urban centers which now control our lives?

It might be simplistic to suggest that our cities alone, by the fact that they physically threaten us, emotionally offend us and socially neglect us, directly cause every social ill. But then again who knows? We do know for certain that a child's personality is largely shaped by his environment, by how it treats him, respects him, responds to him, cares for him; so can we not assume that our stressful, heartless, regimented cities, that "lack any human appeal except . . . bare mechanical order," are going to profoundly affect our personalities as well? Gravely affect how we feel, how we act, and who we are; how needy, how greedy, how callous?

It seems safe to say that callous cities, by and large, breed callous citizens, and the callous citizens build still more callous cities. And this churning eddy of cause, effect, cause, keeps pulling us down until we might all one day be reduced to scavenging in monumental heaps of urban rubble.

We need not be social scientists to comment on what is offensive about city life. We are all experts at it; we live it, we experience it, we feel it, and many of us hate it. Most of us who live in cities spend much of our spare income and thoughts on getting out of them as often as we can. A recent survey found over 50 percent of New Yorkers would move if they could—one assumes financially. (The people of Los Angeles are more complacent but that's probably because they know they could never find their way out.) And it would be redundant to discuss the violence, the crime, the poverty, the filth, jammed freeways, the unbreathable air, relentless noise, relentless pace, impersonal places, numbing jobs, lack of time for family, friends and self, the loneliness, the gruffness; it has all been hashed over a million times before. Perhaps the reaction of an innocent outsider, an Italian peasant woman on her way to visit her American family, sums it all up best. As we flew down through the brown pall that hung over LA, over the endless grid of suburbs slashed by freeways, crushed between overpasses, refineries, parking lots and cars, endless millions of great rivers of cars, she turned to me full of empathy and asked "My God. People live there?"

Benton MacKaye, the father of the Appalachian Trail, felt that for man to lead a wholesome life, in harmony with himself and his world, he would need to have around him towns, wilderness areas, and working farmland. There is no need to stress how absent these things are from average urban life.

That most cities seem, for lack of a better word, inhuman, should come to us as no surprise, for they were not built to glorify or even satisfy their inhabitants, but to facilitate and maximize commerce and profit.

The great migration to the cities came in the first half of the nineteenth century with the boom of the Industrial Revolution. Before that time Europe was "predominantly or overwhelmingly rural" with as much as 70 percent of Prussia, 90 percent of Spain, and 95 percent of Russia living in the country. Cities grew and multiplied once the steam engine made it practical to bring together large concentrations of men, women and children to work in factories. Until then people worked at home or in local workshops close to the water power that propelled the machinery. But the steam engine let entrepreneurs group in urban centers where cheap labor was plentiful, and shipping more cost-efficient. North American cities were no different.

Hence cities were neither founded nor grew because the wisest minds set out to plan an ideal center for human habitation, where individuals and families could thrive and develop in the best possible conditions with the maximum amount of natural beauty, parks, squares, or fresh air. Instead cities were built in fits and starts, with factories, commerce and transportation given priority, and the people squeezed in helter-skelter, where they fit, thereafter.

One need only look around any city to comment honestly on the human condition there. We see fabulous buildings where money is made, great towers where it is kept, glittering shops where it is spent, and clubs and restaurants where it is flashed, and we see a million acres for cars to speed or rest; but where is there space for ordinary people? Where is there inviting space with serenity, greenery, beauty, for mothers to stroll with their infants? And where are the ample clean places to watch toddlers play? Where is there room for children to roam freely without the mortal danger of cars, to explore, to discover, not some pre-produced museum or mechanized exhibit, but the real live natural world, so they can feel it, relate to it at their own pace? Where is there space for spontaneous play? Why do kids die elevator-surfing and intentionally ram patrol cars with cars they have stolen? Where are the schools within a comfortable but stimulating walk from home? Where are the informal places for adolescents to meet other than malls, poolhalls or the fast-food joints? Where can one, during the turbulent years of adolescence, go to find the comforting solitude of Nature? And where can young lovers find seclusion, places of wonder and beauty, where they can experience that fleeting but unique sensation that nothing else matters but each other? Where can neighbors go on strolls and encounter each other casually, spontaneously, and spend time talking, gossiping, being friends? And where can old people spend their precious time, passing on wisdom, being constructive, being a part of society?

To almost every question the modern city answers, "Nowhere."

It has little time or concern for us simple humans, for it is busy hustling and bustling, struggling to get richer, so it can hustle and bustle and struggle even more. But then that is what cities were built for. And just as we can't blame television for its banality so we can't blame cities for their inhumanity, because they were both designed and built solely to make a buck. If that means moronic programs on TV, or crime-filled streets, drugs, violence, social disintegration and an incessant assault on all the senses in the city, well—that's business.

Our suburbs are no better. They were built and designed with the same thought in mind: to give developers and builders the biggest return on their investment. So we have, as Lewis Mumford unforgettably described, "Featureless landscapes of featureless people. A green ghetto, half natural, half plastic, cut off from human contact, where the wife has for her chief daily companions the radio, the soap opera, the refrigerator, the blender, the vacuum cleaner, the washing machine, the dishwasher, and, if she's lucky, the second car." It is a place where the family members gather after work and "together or by turns, immobilize themselves before a television screen, where all that has been left out of the actual world, all their unlived life, flickers before their eyes."

But Mumford left out a few physical facts, such as that suburbs are 50 percent pavement to accommodate the car; that the only large public space is the private mall; that you have to drive five miles to buy a loaf of bread; that in many of them sidewalks are nonexistent; so that, just as in the city, there is little to encourage man to be a friendly, social being.

The result of this is not only that we lead a less vibrant social life but, much more important, that because we live in virtual social isolation, we develop no sense of community, no sense of loyalty, no sense of belonging. Cold proof of that is the Census Bureau's report that 50 percent of Americans changed addresses from 1985 to 1989, and only *nine out of a hundred* of us still live in the same house we lived in in 1960. We still sing "There Is No Place Like Home," but we sing it in a moving van.

We are adrift in our own land. Desperate to be loyal to something, we fervently, sometimes violently, become loyal fans of a local team, one that, laughably enough, is full of players from God-knows-where, who are bought, traded and shipped in and out faster than we can learn their names. That we sense frustration and dislocation should be no surprise. When you add to this economic immobility and TV's constant message of "the good life"—which everybody else but you seems to be leading—, spice it all with the constant "drop dead" message from our cities, the simmering anger and volcanic violence should be no surprise. What *should* surprise us is that there isn't even more.

In three widely separate interviews, one with street-gang leaders in Los Angeles, one with violent young soccer fans in Milan, and one with a neo-Nazi headbuster in Berlin, the identical message was sent blasting to the world: "We are loyal to our cause because nothing in this world is loyal to us."

Maybe the only difference between them and us is that they let their frustration show.

This is not meant as a wholesale condemnation of cities. There is no question that they have brought out some of the best in mankind. Not only did they make possible magnificent architecture, libraries, theaters, museums and much art, but they also acted as havens for artists and intellectuals. But these relatively isolated positives can not be used to justify the much more numerous and more enormous negatives of the modern megalopolis. Smaller cities of old, such as Venice and Florence, gave us infinitely more magnificence per capita without as much dehumanization, without the isolation.

For in cities and in their suburbs we live more or less alone. We seldom know our neighbors. Even my father-in-law, who is retired, and as affable as they come, has managed to meet only two neighbors after ten years in his house. Most often our co-workers are only casual acquaintances, and even friendships tend to be regulated, scheduled events. When we need the help of another human being, be that someone to watch the kids, or fix the door, or just to sit and talk to, we pay. When we need a laugh we rent a movie, when we need security we pay a guard, when we need a friend we pay a shrink.

So in the city we are conditioned, slowly but surely, to think that if we want anything from anyone it is going to cost us *cash*. When we are thus trained to have everything defined in monetary terms, it is understandable that we become vigilant, defensive, always on guard to make sure we get the correct change from Life. And it is also understandable that we try to pay the least for the quickest big return. Since this mentality is pervasive in our society, it is not difficult to see why the cities, ever chasing profit, are having the last drop of blood squeezed out of them now. By all of us. And so bridges crumble, schools self-destruct, and crime spreads like the plague, not because we have too few engineers or teachers or police, but for the much more fundamental reason that we are all too busy fending for ourselves, and as for the rest, well, we just can't give a damn.

If cities want us to care about them, first they will have to first start caring about us. In other words, they will have to consider us at least as important as profits. Diamond lanes and better transport and more police will do nothing. We have to physically change cities, literally break them up into villages no bigger than Greenwich Village, to give us a sense of place, a sense of home again. But changing boundaries on maps and giving cutesy names will have no result at all; the change has to be real. Perhaps we don't have to go to the extreme of the English gentleman's suggestion, who looking down from the Empire State Building on the urban devastation sputtered, "Nothing a little carpet-bombing couldn't mend;" but we have to come pretty close. It's too late to begin building core cities with satellite towns around them; cities and their suburbs are now bigger than galaxies. We literally have to carve away at what we have. With bulldozers. We have to demolish great parts of urban and suburban horror and insert living greenbelts; farmland, parks, and public squares. We have to build communities again. We have to make our schools as airy, as safe and as sacred as our banks; our hospitals as well-staffed and well-served as our bars. We have to help cities feed themselves again from nearby farms and greenhouses instead of transporting every bite a thousand miles. Cars have to go. They have tortured us long enough. They should be put where they belong: stacked one atop another on Henry Ford's bloody grave.

You will smirk and ask "Where will we put the people?" Well if New Yorkers have their druthers half of them will be gone before the day is done. Other cities will empty as soon as (see last chapter) we give support and attention to the country. And where will we get the money? Why not from those who have made trillions in the cities, while they allowed those very cities to crumble under them. If we only reinstate the tax rate for the rich that was in effect in 1979, the sixty thousand Americans who made more than a million dollars a year would donate, in taxes, $40 billion a year. That is about equal to what the federal government budgeted to spend in 1993 on law enforcement, the drug war, courts and prisons, highways, aviation, railroads, mass transit, and the Coast Guard—*combined*.

One can easily imagine how much real structural change that kind of money could bring about in our cities *each year*. Now if we reimposed the 1979 taxes on the almost 800,000 taxpayers who each grossed more than $200,000 a year in 1989, that would yield another $82 billion yearly, or the equivalent of what the Fed budgeted next year for the environment, public lands, agriculture, foreign aid, science and technology (mostly heaving junk into space), commerce, community development, and general government expenses. With a bit of resourcefulness that kind of money could make Palm Beach out of the Bronx. It can be done. It was done in Paris with much success nearly a hundred years ago.

As for manpower, the nation has two million well-paid, able-bodied men and women wasting their lives polishing boots, skipping rope, playing soldiers. Let them go home and rebuild their hometowns instead. Let them smart-bomb Wall Street to let in some fresh air. Let the half-million prisoners wasting away in jails on drug charges—while those who kill 300,000 of us a year with cigarettes sit in the padded box-seats of the sports tournaments and art festivals where they are sponsoring heroes—go home and help rebuild their crumbling neighborhoods. And let America's youth, now dying of boredom at the mall, pitch in a year of community re-building instead. It will do them and us a whole world of good.

Remodeling our sprawling suburbs will be almost painless. Having half of the land paved for the car is an insult to humanity. And the omnipresence of cars dashing down grids of streets precludes relaxed human contact. So why not eliminate traffic from all main streets and let them use the side streets only? We can then convert every block into a hamlet. In front of our homes we can tear up the pavement and plant a village green, dig a pond, have wheat fields, woods and orchards; places where our children can safely roam, neighbors gather, chickens peck. Our driveways and garages would no longer be needed. Half of the one-way side streets would be for communal parking, so the garages could become greenhouses, or Mom and Pop butchers, bakers and candlestick makers. Our driveways will be barnyards. Then as we walk to and from our cars through our village every day, we could get to meet our neighbors, become friends, become civilized social communities again.

Eliminating physical diseases through prevention has been our major and, ultimately, our only successful weapon in the past. All other recent scourges—tuberculosis, malaria, cholera and typhus have been con-trolled primarily through prevention, *not treatment*. Just as malaria was corralled by the draining of swamps, cholera through the cleansing of water, and tuberculosis through the elimination of inhuman dank hovels, so our social ills will have to be cured by eliminating the unlivable swamps of our inner cities, and the unrelievable boredom of the outer. For just as helping those sick with cancer has done nothing to slow its spread, and just as imprisoning whole neighborhoods has not slowed the use of drugs, so petty handouts of a few dollars more a month, or short-term social programs, or activity centers, will do nothing but temporarily slow society's fall. But we will certainly make inroads if we start with the acknowledgement that, by and large, our cities, measured by most social, environmental, and reasonable human standards, are unfit for habitation. And while our suburbs may mostly satisfy our need for physical security, they do nothing to satisfy our social human needs; they do nothing to encourage us to be anything but strangers who happen to park their cars on the same street every night.

Of course embarking on a rebuilding—or demolishing—venture of this scale would mean changing our priorities. They're a bore anyway. And it would mean changing our plans for the future, although I'm not sure we have any. Or we can wait. We can wait until the fire spreads slowly from L.A. and does the demolishing for us. And we don't have to just open our wallets and give freely; we can wait until they're taken from us with a gun. We might change our minds then, except we might be dead.

11

HUMANE
SMALL TOWNS

*There they were out in the fields with their kids, the
happiest, most solid families you can imagine.*
　　　　　—Dr. John Fraser Hart
　　　　　　　Author; Professor of Geography

*My only regret is not doing it sooner. I wish I could
have given my kids what I'm giving my grandchildren,
working with them on the herbs. The country is falling
apart, and this is a way to keep families together.*
　　　　　—Leroy Wilton, 53.
　　　　　　　Laid-off steelworker; now herb grower

No one has to tell us about the pleasures of a small town. We know them well, if not from reality then from the old Andy Griffith show, or *It's a Wonderful Life*. But the small town we know the best is the one deep in our heart, with its elm-shaded streets, little clapboard houses and picket fences, and gnarled fruit trees and run-amok vegetable gardens, where doors are never locked, and where shop-keepers stand in front of their shops and greet you, and the cop greets you, all by name, and you stop and chat with them because what else is life for, and when the bells toll at noon the shops close up, and you all go home for lunch, a nap, then out to hoe the melons or to do a little fishing; and everyone you liked in fourth grade is still your friend, and it's a swell place to be a kid and perfect to be a family, and it's a humane place to grow old, and, when you have to go, it's a good place to die.

If such a town doesn't exist, the big question is "Why?" If we all dream about it, if we all long for it—and recent surveys found seven out of ten of us would live there if we could—then where in damnation is it? When all it takes is a few good-natured people; a few to teach school, a few to own the stores, some to farm the land, some to mend the sick and a bar to tend the healthy, then *why* isn't there such a town behind every tree? I mean only a few of us dream of having missiles, tanks, and bombers, and rockets to the moon, yet the world is littered with them; hardly anyone dreams of pesticides and freeways, yet they're choking us to death; no one dreams of junk mail, yet we're drowning in the stuff; no one I know dreams of stripmalls and fast-food chains, yet there are a hundred to a mile! How the hell did it happen that the things hardly any of us want are burying us all, while the simple town we all dream of we can rarely find?

What is all this?!—Really!

How did we let the one thing that was the very cornerstone of North America's culture, both native and thereafter, its oldest, proudest, most socially perfect heritage, vanish? Perhaps some of the truth is that the snake-oil salesmen got to us all and sold us new and improved progress; a thousand flashy gadgets that not only closed the local craftsmen's doors, but made us all less dependent on each other, so little by little we drifted apart. Then there were the absentee landlords, not just the kind that drove sharecroppers from the land, but also the weekend kind that bought out Jim Davis's neighbors, and the great impersonal God-knows-who-owned chains and malls—none of them built in aid of humanity but as tax-deferring "investments" for the rich—that helped kill Main Street and forced the family-owned-and-cared-for business out of business; Charley's Garage, the general store, the drugstore, the luncheonette, the movie house, the butcher, the baker and even the grocer.

But the larger and even sadder part of the truth is that we abandoned our small towns for the bright lights of the cities; the mythical steady jobs, the excitement, the fun people, often to find the steady job unsteady, the excitement fake, and most of the people as interesting as the sidewalk. Many of us would like to return to the country, but cite a dozen obscure reasons why we can't, when in truth our biggest fear is "How will I survive?" Dumb. For while it is true that cash in country life can be sporadic, even scarce, you must consider just how little of it you need compared to living in the city.

In cities and suburbs we live among strangers and have to pay in cold cash for any help that we receive. In small towns, on the other hand, we know all our neighbors, and while this results in as many enemies as friends, at least we have the joy of *knowing* those we hate, with the near miraculous bonus of often knowing *why*. This privilege in the city costs you ten years of weekly therapy at a hundred bucks an hour plus cab fare.

So, while in a city we have to pay carpenters, baby sitters, cabbies, shrinks and nurses, in a small town we can usually coerce some neighbor, tenth cousin or friend to play the role for free. Of course we might then, depending on our upbringing, be consumed with guilt and indebtedness, but this is not all bad, for it will give us something to fret about on long dark winter nights.

One of the greatest advantages of country life is that it allows room, both physical and emotional, for multi-generation families. In Tuscany it is almost unthinkable to have grandmothers and grandfathers live alone, and they often turn out to be, as eighty-year old Nonna is at the Paoluccis, the wisest, most stable and arguably the most productive members of the family. This is a far cry from the many seniors of North America who often live lives of desperate isolation.

Country folk thus develop a quiet interdependence, helping each other, knowing that the help they give today, they'll need and get tomorrow. The important part of this is not just that it costs less to survive in the country. Few would question that. But we gain a certain calm in knowing that care and help are all around, and—a thing just as vital—knowing that our support and caring are needed by others.

So what? say the skeptics. Well, so everything. When we help each other directly, personally, without monetary gain, we get to know each other better, become better friends. And the more we help and care, the more reflexive these actions then become, until they develop into a constant way of thinking, a way of looking at our neighbors and the world; a way of life that stays with us like our skin or, dare I say, our hearts. I don't think I need to convince city dwellers how absent this quality is from average city life.

And just as we get to know people in the country, so we get to know the country itself. Not in theory or from pictures, but firsthand. We get to know *a* tree, get to know its shade on a scorching summer's day, or its shape against a reddening sky; how good it is for footholds or a fort, or how good its fruit is to eat or to throw at passing dogs. And we get to know *a* creek, the rocks on its bottom, the taste of its water, its fishing holes, its swimming holes. And that tree and that creek can become as important to our lives as are our neighbors, and just as we can see the results of our actions—good or bad—on their faces, so we will learn to see the results of the good or harm we do a creek or a tree. And the pain we cause them we will feel ourselves, as any child who has broken a sapling or killed a bird knows well. Then we might think and care more about the things we do, the damage we can cause; might even worry about each can of oil we dump, the bug killer we spray, each gallon of gas we burn, the useless junk we buy—each thoughtless injury we inflict on our world.

So where was I? Oh yes, money.

The largest single expense in the country will of course be the farm, which can be as small as five acres to feed your family and sell a little something on the side. If you want more self-reliance, try for twenty, half in woods for firewood and lumber and peace of mind, half in fields for orchards and for crops. Twenty acres may not sound like much, but when you consider that on three acres you can grow enough vegetables to feed fifty families of vegetarians, then it's a lot. Anyway, whereas in the city $100,000 buys but a frugal one-bedroom apartment or in the suburbs an empty lot, the same sum in farming country will get you a good older house with twenty acres and a barn. Or if you want seclusion how about this one: "3 BR rustic. 240 acres secluded Canadian lake, 40 miles from Kingston, Ontario (a smallish city). Dock, sandy beach, propane and solar 12V system. Ideal naturalist area, abundant fish, geese, ducks. $110,000."

But big savings in country living continue thereafter and go well beyond the obvious, growing and preserving food. Take for example transportation. Since any city job almost always includes commuting, a predictable expense will be The Car. Because punctuality is an accepted curse with most jobs, an inexpensive but reliable old beater might have done us, but since city culture is centered upon keeping ahead of the Joneses, we tend to buy cars that hurtle us within a gnat's hair of bankruptcy.

In the country, on the other hand, the less flashy our car, the less stupid the neighbors tend to think us to be. A rusty, wired-together pickup is the epitome of fashion. This at a blink can save you ten to twenty grand. Initially. For in the city you are considered subversive unless you trade in, and up, every couple of years. With car payments, interest, maintenance, insurance, depreciation and the occasional fender-bender, city slickers can easily fritter away $5,000 a year just on the heap.

Then there are clothes. In our service society more and more jobs are white-collar. This means clothes. Lots of them, for most of us would rather die a painful death than wear the same thing to work two days in a row. And night and weekend clothes simply know no bounds. What is worse, our clothes, like our cars, are seldom discarded because of wear and tear, but simply because they have gone out of some laughable thing called fashion. While it is impossible to set an average outlay for city clothes, a survey of New York friends revealed that, even though many of them worked in publishing where unpretentious dressing is a matter of tradition, and in spite of much bargain hunting, $2,000 a year seemed to be the bottom of a scale that knew no top. There were two women who grudgingly admitted to $5,000, and one insurance executive who confessed to ten. Now that is a lot of loot compared to the country where you can get by with a couple of shirts, wear the same jeans or skirts for five years and the same jacket for twenty, and stylish, flashy clothes look about as fitting as panties on a cow.

Most things that we have to buy can cost less in the country. Furniture, carpets, pottery, even clothes, are still—or again—being made by craftsmen. Since most purchases are direct, you eliminate all the middlemen who normally stand between you and the machine. But there are two even more important things. First, there is the quality. Craftsmen normally put their hearts and souls into their work, making everything as well as they possibly can, meaning that what they make might just last your lifetime, whereas the mass-produced thing might be in the landfill before the year is out. And second is the emotional tie. In a craftsman-made object you can feel the work of a human being, see a thought here, a care there, and even if it wasn't crafted specially for you, though it often is, through that human contact it seems to have a life. To discard it and replace it would be somewhat like trading in a friend.

Another unavoidable city expense is personal maintenance. This means glitzing up your outside to hide how
dull you are. And while your outside glitters, your brain
clouds and your soul atrophies. You can of course argue
that a new hairdo will attract approval, temporarily calming your fears, and thus aiding your mental health; but a
new hairdo is new but once a month so what will shore
you up for the other thirty days? Feel-good placebos are
nearly inexhaustible, from manicures to body-building
to having face and body parts moved to what seem like
better places, all triggered by a weak self-identity, something readily cured in the country by planting a few
potatoes, chopping some wood, going next door for a
cup of tea, or going for a quiet walk to watch the sun go
down. For free.

Then there is the expense of maintaining physical
health. In the country you eat better, sleep better, relax
better, and thus stay incomparably more healthy. Sick
people in the city are often sent to recover in the country,
but *never* vice versa. And, in the country, exercise is endless—everything from working the garden to chopping
wood, to building and toting—and not only are they
free, but they actually bring in money or cut expenses.

Much spare cash in the city goes for entertainment, the
diversions needed to forget the gloom of city life. As
cities stagger under the combined crises of unmanaged
growth, pollution, and poverty, not only does the need
for diversion intensify, but so does the cost, for one has to
travel farther to find even the simplest of pleasures like a
quiet walk, or a sit in the park. So those seeking escapes
have no choice but to pay. Dearly.

The most popular and most costly city entertainment is
going to the country. Indeed the best thing most cities

offer is a chance to get the hell out of them. Because of the almost limitless variety of escapes, ranging from a week-end at an inn to the $300,000 beach house, the average cost is impossible to ascertain, but it is safe to say that it is an expense most country folk can happily forgo.

Then there are incidental nights out. Dinner for two in even a modest restaurant will cost you sixty dollars. If you throw in a concert, performance, or play, you can kiss another fifty to a hundred bucks good-bye. So at best you are out a hundred dollars, at worse a whole lot more, and you have spent an evening among strangers, felt a little thrill, but you are probably no closer to humanity than when the evening started.

In the country things are different. Entertainment money you don't need, just imagination. First and fore-most there are friends. When there are few paid-for dis-tractions your friends become more dear. Few things are as nurturing as an evening at the Paoluccis', sipping wine; watching Nonna sew, Eleanora do homework, the fire; talking about the farm, about the wind, about who was born, who died, the feasts thereafter, the memories, the loss, things that are dear to you, close to you. And at the end of it we walk home, feeling the wine, on the dark ridge-road under the stars, and sense some kind of contact with it all—the Paoluccis, the silent valley, the animals in the stalls, the warmth of the summer night. You feel that you belong.

We lived in a mountain village once on Canada's west coast where twenty feet of snow fell every winter, and at night we walked on the wind-swept frozen lake with the moon bright and the snow as white as day, and the mountains glistening and the soft wind whispering and blowing snow around our feet across the ice. And we played hockey on the frozen lake during the day, kids, girls, women, men, no organizing, no set teams, boots for goalposts, and fresh air, and skates gleaming in the low sun, and the long walk home on wobbly legs. In the evening we had theater. Live. Our own.

We started a theater in the old school there, ten of us, all grown, no experience, no stage, no sets, no lights, and we did plays by Beckett, and Pinter, and Albee, and few of us knew who they were and nobody really cared. We knew little about blocking or motivations, but had no inhibitions or pretensions, and the muscles behind our ears hurt from laughing at our own audacity, at intonations no one ever dreamed of and often wished they had never made. When we performed for the village everybody came and saw the set made with old sheets and bent work lamps from our basements, and those nights were as vibrant and full of life as Sam Shepherd in New York or the Bolshoi in the Louvre courtyard. And even better still because we were among friends.

There is one other thing about entertainment in the country. Just as you are responsible for the work in your stalls and fields, so you are responsible for creating your own fun. And just as the satisfaction gained from working for yourself, with your own hands, is almost beyond compare, so will be the fun you dream up and create on your own. Just as watching any World Series pales when compared to playing softball with your friends, so most store-bought entertainment fades and is forgotten; while an afternoon spent fishing at a stream with family, or a solitary moonlight walk in fresh snow-covered fields will stay vivid in your memory until the day you die. I'm not sure you can ask any more of life.

12

THE DEATH
OF THE INDIVIDUAL
Mechanical Lovers,
Electronic Friends

*We fill the hands and nurseries of our children with all
manner of dolls, drums and horses, withdrawing their
eyes from the plain face and . . . Nature, the sun and
moon, the animals, the water and stones which should be
their toys.* —Emerson

One of the cornerstones of North American civilization
has always been the worship of individualism. We had a
whole continent to roam, and we had the freedom to alter
it the way we thought it best. We had no past restricting
us. We simply pushed aside those who lived here before,
so we had only a future. Europe, reined in by ancient
cultures and traditions, and lack of space, always had a

more limited view; individualism was often stifled by history. So not only adventurers and fortune hunters found paradise here, but so did scientists and artists. The pioneer, the discoverer, the Brave Loner who looks at the world from his own measured viewpoint and makes it bow to him is still our hero. At the movies. For in truth, we are the largest flock of neatly herded sheep that ever tore a green pasture to shreds. Don't feel insulted; I'm right here bahing with you.

As I said about our houses, we did once have a choice, many choices, but we have let them slip away, to the point where it would be difficult to live the life we want *even if we knew* what it was we wanted. And this is the saddest part. The herding starts so early, is so thoroughly complete by the time we are of age, that we don't even begin to question anymore because, as with the taste of a *real* tomato or the peace of quiet Sundays, we have forgotten what it is we're missing.

We condemn our children to conformity the minute they leave the womb. And we do so not from unkindness, but because we have thoughtlessly built ourselves a media-propelled society that for the last forty years has bludgeoned us every minute, telling us to forget that we are humans who need to laugh and cry, care and be cared for, love and be loved. It tells us instead that our needs can be fulfilled with storebought goods; that having video games is as good as having friends, that the comfort of your car can replace the comfort of your lover, that caring for a yacht is like caring for your mother, and that new shoes can substitute for a shoulder to cry on.

So we created a society that bloomed economically the farther it pushed us apart, because the lonelier we got the more we shopped to forget our loneliness; a society that reached its apex once it convinced us that bells and whistles, car phones and Nintendos can make up for the loss of a passionate human life.

This of course should come as no surprise, since we are a society named not after something noble or humane, but an abstract vulgarity called Capital. We have become conditioned to ignore the growth of the human spirit, or human joy, or at least to practice them in our spare time, and concentrate our efforts on the growth of *money*. It is somehow thought (if it is thought about at all) that happiness, fulfillment, love and laughter will burst upon us as soon as we are adequately awash in a sea of greenbacks.

But back to our children. In this goods-driven culture, we prepare them from birth for a life rich in physical comforts but bereft of love. We give them all that money can buy but we won't give them our time. We shower them with Ninja Turtles, phones, and VCRs, but shortchange them on companionship. The result is that, according to the 1991 Carnegie Foundation report, our children grow up "burdened with inattentive or overworked parents . . . mindless television programming and isolation from adults." A bleak childhood at best.

I'm sure we can all think of examples but here is one anyway. A professional couple, gentle, cultured, travelled, had their first child. They were thrilled. But after eight weeks the mother had to return to work. Both parents worked long hours. Before she started school the child went through *ten* nannies. Why the nannies kept leaving is of little import, but what we saw in our visit to their house was a bright, intelligent child smashing burning firewood against the kitchen wall, a child throwing rocks at us when we skated with her, and one who spent the last fifteen minutes of waiting for a train trying gleefully to push Mommy onto the tracks.

When I related the particulars of the story to a child psychologist friend, he told me the child was desperate for discipline and love, reaching out to a world that would give her neither.

The parents deserve only part of the blame. They, as us all, are so overwhelmed every minute by this relentless world of work-hype-run-change-buy, that, not having the luxury of time to reflect, to make real choices, grab onto whatever garbage truck rumbles by and proceed to call that Life.

Not only do we allow our children to roam alone through this joyless, mindless labyrinth-of-junk culture—even Dante had someone directing him through Hell—but we, having ourselves become happy charter members, actually encourage them to indulge. Not only do we *not* use the horrors of mass consumption as punishment, but we hold them up as ideals. If the world were as it should be, we would be *punishing* our children by taking them to the mall, not *rewarding* them with it, much as in Sir Thomas More's *Utopia* it was the "criminals who . . . are forced to wear golden rings . . . golden bands . . . chains . . . and even gold crowns on their heads."

But then this ain't no Utopia.

So instead of teaching our children modesty, we inadvertently teach them to exhibit what they own; instead of teaching them wisdom we fill their minds with facts; instead of teaching them how to share we teach them how to hoard. And all their fine possessions leave them little room to imagine, almost no need to fantasize and no need to invent. And that leaves us, by and large, with a legion of clone-like young who, numbed "by our failure to stimulate their minds," while sporting unique haircuts, are frighteningly homogeneous in their lack of spirit, vision, and dreams.

When we inundate our children with junk toys and junk knowledge, we bury one of life's great treasures—mystery. When, with well-intentioned kindness, we deluge them with things that clang bang spin flash scream burp whine—the blatant, the sensational—we numb them to the myriad subtleties of their fellow humans and the natural world around them. By constantly so distracting them, we discourage them from observing and interpreting the world and people for themselves. So the importance of humanity and nature is diminished in their eyes. Human expression, human behavior, as well as the miracles of ever-changing nature, woods, creeks, oceans, meadows and bogs, hold little if any fascination. What fascinates is the new toy and new gear. And since that toy is identical from coast to coast, since all entertainment is identical from coast to coast, we end up with a continent of the predictably mundane, where individuality is no longer even rumor.

Most child psychologists agree that every time we give a child a toy we prevent him from inventing it. We have all heard this line a hundred times, so why do we keep buying our children all this rubbish?

Many of us try to do good by giving them educational toys whose circles fit here and squares fit there, where if you yank this a light goes on, and if you push that a door pops open. Educational?! Sure, it gives them a sense of control over their mechanical world, but it brings them no closer to the family of man. We are not teaching them to be pensive, insightful human beings; we are teaching them to keep busy. We don't emphasize the need to understand humanity, we emphasize the importance of understanding gadgets. We don't teach them to be creative, or outrageous, or help enrich their minds, but how to follow step-by-step instructions, how to perfect hand-eye coordination; how to become assembly line fodder. How to become full-fledged members at The Mall. We are teaching them to *baah*.

With all these well-equipped but unimaginative drones, who is going to lead humanity? Or understand humanity? Or help humanity or even look at a simple human face instead of Nintendo? I mean what chance does a poor human being who merely talks, smiles and cries have against a screen that flashes, explodes and crashes fifty times a second? On command! All he has to do is twitch his nervous little finger. All Nintendo tells a kid is that humanity is dull and machines are as wonderful as the world can ever be. It is teaching him to want mechanical lovers and electronic friends.

We look after our children's little brand-name clothes and fluorescent jogging gear, and take them to kiddy gym and buy them kid's perfume and every video game every huckster ever dreamed up, but what about their minds? And, excuse me if I'm maudlin, but what about their souls?

I know I'm prone to generalize and am first to admit that I'm basing my comments on casual observations, but after twenty-five years of travel I think this is fairly true. In any poor country, from the poorer parts of Ireland and Hungary, to China, Burma, or Mexico where children rarely have a toy—educational or otherwise—to call their own, with shacks for homes, dirt for floors, rags for clothes and rice and beans for dinner year in and year out, their eyes glow full of life. They sparkle. They're excited. Bursting with the sense that at any second something marvelous may happen. They are thrilled to be alive; thrilled just to be children. To be among them is an inebriating joy.

I'm not trying to romanticize their poverty. It has horrible aspects, but they do know a joy, a sense of wonder, that most well-off children were deprived of at an early age. They know that when you have no *things,* then the whole world is your toy. Or can be. Has to be. I've watched children play for hours with a stick, or a barrel-stave, or rocks, or just dirt. They didn't have to worry about what piece went where; anything went anywhere. It is true that when they grow up they might make lousy computer programmers, or undisciplined factory workers, or even bad executives, but by God, they make great people. And, for now, even greater kids.

I don't think I have to push the comparison between them and the many mostly bored, often edgy, toy-laden children in our affluent society. And the saddest part is that we meant so well. We ate the advertising with a spoon.

But there is a special kind of toy that you can provide. The one you make yourself. It may not look as slick as the store-bought one, but to your child that won't matter. What will matter is that you took the time, made the effort, and poured in all the creative power, love and care that you could muster. That toy will keep on living long after it's gone, and long after you're gone, because he will pass on to his children all the love that you put in it. My grandfather made me some toys—a little wooden castle, a plywood rocking horse—and the love he made those with bolsters me to this day.

Now I know that one kid's experience will not help found a theory, but I can tell you, now that my poor parents are dead and this won't hurt their feelings, that the toys that were the most expensive, the ones they struggled hardest with their meager earnings to provide, turned out to be, for me, the dullest of them all. There was the electric train set. I was beside myself with joy and thought I had just made Heaven, but the fun of watching that thing buzz around in circles wore off in a week.

Then there was the chemistry set with twenty jars of goodies, test-tubes, Bunsen burner, magnesium strips, manual, and microscope. I used them but a handful of times, once to nearly kill the landlord with sulphur gas, and once to turn a jar of pure clear liquid red. As for the microscope, I used it once, on Billy Evans's insistence, when I tried to find the pecker on a fly.

I had infinitely more fun building a moated and walled town behind the compost box in good mud with a spoon. That lasted for months. You could tear it down and mush it around and add sticks and pebbles and reeds and branches and pour in real water and carve little boats with paper sails that moved when you blew them. And there was never a question of how it was supposed to look; there were no instructions; everything that happened to that heap of mud came from inside me. It was my own, done the way I felt it should be done, done the way that small world fit my dreams.

And I spent weeks turning the boring, white side of the grocery store—the side that faced the woods of our backyard—into the main street of a Western town. I painted a bank, sheriff's office, saloon, general store, brothel and a church, even painted Boot Hill with some crosses. It was no work of art, as I was loudly told later by my parents and the owner, but what can you expect from a half-gallon of old paint and a worn whiskbroom?

Anyway, how well it was painted was not the point. I didn't do it for others to see or because I had a passion to paint. I did it so I could have a western town to play in. And not only did I learn to populate a whole town from my imagination—the place was so full of people you could barely move—but I also learned that I could, with almost nothing, look after and entertain myself. And that I could make, from nothing, my own toys and my own world. When we teach our children reliance on store-bought goods, we rob them of the chance of *self*-reliance; and when we take away the need to create, we rob them of the chance to practice their uniqueness, their individuality.

For it is not only the number of gadgets that clutter our children's brain, but the rigid specificity of today's toys that is so limiting. Take, for example, a simple doll. Not long ago girls might receive a doll made by a relative or friend. If store-bought, it was an innocuous-looking thing upon which she could bestow a name, a personality, likes and dislikes, needs and wants. She could decide what words it might intimately whisper just to her. In other words, that doll could become an extension of herself, whatever her *own* imagination wanted it to be. Today's dolls are different. Most are pre-named, have a rigid set of clothing for every occasion (the more the maker can sell you down the road) and they cry and pee and say mechanical, predictably dull words. And they don't come alone.

Barbie, perhaps the most famous of them all, of whom *five* were sold for *every American child born since 1960*, comes with various houses; a mansion for a cool $350, a musical house for only $200, or an Amazing RV for only

$89. We no longer have a simple rocking horse or truck, a puppet, or a doll we can bring to life ourselves. We have specific horses, trucks, figures, and dolls that come from the factory complete with names, personalities, and known behavior. As with the infinite number of Ninja Turtle figures, we are told by the publicity men the age, sex, good or bad behavior, occupation, and purpose of each. In other words, the toy comes complete with a regimented world. So complete that there is no room for the child; no room for his needs, his dreams, no room for his waning, ebbing imagination.

It is losses such as these, tiny but adding up, that we undergo by the hundreds in a world where the emphasis is on the possession of mass-made streams of junk. And it is the loss of this *specialness* that we feel the most, that turns every day into a mundane drone. For if the world spins so quickly, tells us every second what we are to be, what we are to do, what we are to wish for, what we are to think, then when do we have time to really be ourselves? When do we have time to become the noble individual we have the potential to be? And if the world is so full of instructions, be they as subtle as a regimented toy or a picture of a pretty woman selling you a car, then where is there room for us? In a world that's full of toys, who are we, really? And in a world so full of toys, who has time to care?

13

LOSING OUR CHILDREN

America is losing sight of its children. In decisions made every day we are placing them at the very bottom of our agenda with grave consequences for the future of the nation.
—A Carnegie Foundation Report

The current ratio of the average salary of an American CEO to that of an American public school teacher: 73 to 1.
—Harpers—U.S. Department of Labor

I have difficulty determining what our society is about. I mean, if our children are placed "at the very bottom of our agenda," what on earth do we value more than them? What are our priorities? What do we live for? What gives us pride? I remember the prelude to the Gulf War, when a letter to the editor was full of admiration for the rapid deployment of troops and equipment. The writer said, "For the first time in a long time I feel proud." Is that it then? Are we proud of having a prompt delivery service? Will that round out our legacy to our children—a devastated environment, a lifetime's worth of debt, and efficient take-out?

In report after report, one reads about the dismal performance of our children, their lack of abilities and skills, their lack of interest. The general findings were succinctly summarized by Christopher T. Cross, assistant secretary of education: "The bottom line is that very few American students demonstrate they can use their minds well."

Why?

It can't be for lack of input; our whole society is one big Disneyland. Or for lack of information, we are drowning in the stuff. Is it the lead in the water? Or is it simply that no one gives a damn?

I am not sure what most of us consider the foundation of our society, or what we think will determine our future, but how can anything be more important than our children? If for no other than purely selfish reasons, we should nurture them much better. Do you want, in your old age, to be treated by a doctor who cannot use his mind? And does any CEO want to have to pick his team from a brain-dead pool of toads?

That we are abandoning them there can be no doubt. As Jane Gross observed in her *New York Times* essay early last year: "Young people . . . have been the subject of dozens of national studies, learned reports and civic jeremiads in recent months, all deploring the conditions of life for many of the 64 million children of America, particularly the 13 million who are poor." And she quotes Dr. Joyce Lashof, president of the American Public Health Association: "What we are seeing is the complete destruction of the social environment for these kids. Economic opportunity, stable relationships, housing, safety at school, hope for the future: Everything that makes up living has kind of disappeared for them."

And for those who need concrete proof, Jane Gross cites a terrifying statistic: "A threefold increase in homicide and suicide rates among teenagers in the last thirty years, which experts say signals the depth of their despair about the future."

What is the matter with us?

How could we have so neglected our children? Have we become completely heartless or just insensitive to their needs? And if we say that we would like to care but are simply too busy, I'd have to ask immediately: "Busy doing what? Paying off the mortgage on a yet bigger house? Or a new car, or a giant TV?" Don't we know yet that it is *us* our kids need; our time, our love, our understanding, our care? They would live happily in a shack if we just gave them more of ourselves. Before all else, and above all else, we have to show our children that they have a place in our world. That they are cared about. That they belong.

A recent Department of Education report was released after extensively surveying 9 million school kids. Eighth graders were asked how often in the last six months they had talked to a parent about their schoolwork. Half of them responded, "Once or twice, or not at all." And one-third responded, "Never." This is madness. What *do* we talk to them about? Haircuts? Sunglasses? Somebody's latest facial relocation? Do we talk at all? Or have we simply, under the relentless, crushing demand of longer and longer hours of commuting and work, and the grueling task of keeping up premises and appearances, become completely deaf and dumb, save for our prerecorded patter about the weather, baseball scores, and new weeds in the lawn. Have we taken a cue from junk bonds, junk food, junk mail, and junked our minds as well?

It is no mystery where our children learned not to use their minds: from us. According to a 1988 National Geographic survey, fully half of all Americans didn't know that the then Soviet Union was in the Warsaw Pact. In fact, one out of ten actually believed that America was. Six out of ten did not know the population of the United States, and half of them didn't know that Contras and Sandinistas had been fighting in Nicaragua. Now these might not have been life-and-death issues to them, but when the government had been spending nearly half of their tax dollars protecting them from the Warsaw Pact and the Sandinista devils, one would think that, if nothing else, simple curiosity about where their money is being flushed would keep them in touch with the outside world. The rest of their ignorance our children picked up on their own. They never had to think. From earliest childhood they have been *told* everything by television, advertising, teachers, and politicians.

There is no doubt that the job of revamping our education system is urgent and enormous. But, contrary to much current thinking, the solution doesn't lie in leaner school curriculums, interschool competition, bringing more computers into classes, or even in supplying niftily packaged ten-minute TV news broadcasts complete with two minutes of much flashier commercials. That is merely cleaning windows when the building is falling down. The society outside the school, our home life, neighborhood life, our whole cultural emphasis, has infinitely more bearing on how our children will do in school than whether they use PCs or blackboards or write in the dirt with sticks. In fact, even a new Department of Education report places most of the blame for the mediocrity of American schooling *outside* the school system. After chiding some educators and administrators for using "outmoded passive teaching methods," the report lays blame on both parents and the community—meaning the country at large—for being uninvolved in our children's education. And the recommendations of the Carnegie report, which found "35 percent of students started school unprepared to learn," are equally broad-based, ranging from job-sharing and more flexible hours for parents, to less mindless children's television programs, more parks, kids' tours for a broad range of stimulation, closed streets for safe play, and more adult contact and involvement. So the changes needed are profound. We will have to, as Lewis Mumford said, "Begin all over again at the very beginning, with the infant in its crib. That is where education starts."

Strangely enough, it is in the crib that our society begins to reject us. To illustrate how warped and child-excluding our world tends to be, I will subject you to but a single anecdote. One evening we went out to dinner with friends in Newport, California, to a simple, unpretentious place. We sat, ordered, and while waiting for the food, the baby began making hungry sounds. So, Renée, as was her custom, opened her blouse and started to feed him. The baby had taken only a couple of gulps when the manager, alerted by the waitress, rushed over flushed, part embarrassed, part angry, and blurted—I swear that this is true—"I'm sorry Ma'am, you can't do that here. This is a family restaurant."

Are we nuts?!

What on earth can be more family than a mother feeding her babe?! Can that somehow be offensive? It is perfectly acceptable to have some three-hundred pound slob snort and slobber while he gnaws the still-bloody flesh of some half-dead animal, but it is taboo for a baby to drink from his mother's breast?! Even if we're the most rigid puritans, haven't we ever seen religious paintings? Breasts galore!

There is no doubt that we have a society standing on its head. How else could the guy who makes neckties or eyeshadow earn *seventy-three times more* than the person who shapes our children's minds? Not only should we tolerate babes and children and all their needs, but we should make their fulfillment our priority. We should move them from "the very bottom of the agenda" to the very top. Not only should we create a niche for them, but we should design and plan our world around them. The only concentrated attention our children get now is when someone is trying to sell them something. Then "Kiddie World" blooms. Kiddie restaurants, kiddie parks and kiddie gyms sprout like mushrooms in the rain. Some claim this gives children a sense of independence, their own world, and of course that is true. But it is a warped, tiny, desiccated world, where everything is Day-Glo and everybody smiles and nothing is ever wrong. It is a world cut off from the grown-up one, cut off from the variety of adults with a variety of problems, and often a variety of ways of solving them. They will miss out on arguing, reasoning, developing ideas, developing viewpoints; using their minds. The adult world might at times be confusing, unpleasant, and even wrought with pain, but just as often it can be filled with laughter, or love, or concern and caring. And whatever else it will be, it will be rich in complexity and emotion, and will give children not only an understanding and appreciation of their own species, but, just as important, a sense of inclusion in it.

And this varied human contact may possibly kindle their interest in humans. Not the robot-like dribblers, smilers and screamers on TV, with their fake, simplistic response to fake, dumb situations, but real, unscripted humans. And among this fragile, joyous lot they might find some heroes, not the cardboard superheroes in whom their kiddie world abounds, but vulnerable, ever-changing, puzzling, messy humans, whom you can hate like hell one minute and love like hell the next, who might just give them some ideas of what they might like, and not like, to grow up to be. And they might then grow up with a more rounded, deeper view of things, and might learn to look for, and find, a better life in this warped world.

And we should not give them a world that divides us into easy-to-market-to compartments, putting teenagers here, grownups there, old folks in the attic. Because the most formative, most profound and most lasting things in life, we will, without fail, learn *not* from books or videos or computers or classes, but from each other. In other words, it takes people to teach people to be people. And the more varied those people can be in age, character, background, views and needs, the richer will be our learning, the deeper our understanding, and the more unquenchable our thirst for wanting to learn more.

I think it is fair to say that our children perform poorly in school, and "cannot use their minds," not because they lack the physiological pieces or the technical gadgets, but because they lack the curiosity, the interest to learn. And why should they want to? Why should they be interested in the world when all their lives the world has shown no real interest in them?

And why should they yearn for insight and knowledge when they live in a fatuous world obsessed with fame and fortune, where social and financial success goes to those to whom education was the least of their concerns—sports stars, rock stars and entrepreneurs—where intelligence and broad learning are, if anything, a guarantee of being left behind; and where even the president of the country believes "the vision thing" to be an option in life like whitewall tires on a car. It is little wonder then that most of our kids are just putting in time, counting on their Swatches the minutes to the mall.

The sad part is that over the last thirty years, many of those who still show an interest in learning do so more and more merely for extraneous reasons—to pass tests, to get a diploma—rather than to enjoy broadening their minds, gaining wisdom. And here I talk about what was for me the most enjoyable of subjects, English literature, which was like story-telling on school time. A revealing editorial by William Clayton, an English teacher in high school and adjunct college professor for thirty-five years, relates that he has seen "students become increasingly dependent on such trots as Monarch and Cliffs notes." (For those who have been away too long, these are "explanations" of pieces of literature, containing outlines of, and comments on, the work.) He says that these notes are no longer read only to help explain the more difficult pieces, but are read *instead* of such accessible titles as *Animal Farm* and Steinbeck's *The Pearl*. And the Department of Education report concurs: "Few students read much or analytically."

In other words, our children are not learning to think, they are simply perfecting the act of transferring information from one piece of paper to another without putting any of themselves in between. They are not learning to form opinions or gain experience, feel passions or even make interpretations; they rely on all the answers from outside. It is no wonder that they grow up to accept the most mind-numbing careers, and elect the most half-witted politicians, because they're used to doing as they are told; they have taught themselves that the answers lie in someone else's condensed view of life.

Just one last anecdote.

During my last year of university I substitute-taught high school to get by. Taught everything from Spanish (my total knowledge was "Eso es un robo", which I learned from *Butch Cassidy* and means "This is a holdup") to senior girls' phys. ed., where I barely knew where to look. And I taught some English.

One day I got grade nines who were almost finished reading *The Lord of the Flies*. We read and talked and I looked at the questions the *real* teacher had left for her students. One question was, "Who was the Lord of the Flies?" And she wrote the answer down. I asked the class. Hands flew up. I picked the scholarly-looking kid and of course his answer was "right." I said so. The class went silent. I was about to move on to the next question when a street-wise-looking kid thrust his hand up in the air. He gave another answer. For once in my life I had the wisdom to keep my mouth shut. Then I asked him to explain. He did, with rough syntax but clear and bright reasoning. I was floored. More hands shot up and the class began to buzz. Hands waved, words flew and faces got excited. They explained, they argued. Almost every one of those little guys had an answer, a *different* answer, his *own* answer, from his *own* mind, his *own* heart, his *own* interpretation, his *own* life! The hell with official schoolnotes, the hell with William Golding! *They* had read the book, *they* had thought it through, *they* had felt it through, and *they knew!* And by God they were right and no one else was going to tell them different! I had seldom felt so alive. And I felt honored to be with them. That was in 1969.

I think most of us agree that fundamental social changes have to come. But those will take time. There are changes that we need to make at once before another generation of our children wastes away. Major social and physical menaces have bloomed in our society these last few decades to which our schools have reacted barely at all, while at the same time they have embraced all technical innovation as the newest savior. These threats have to be addressed and countered and the earlier we start the better. Call them Survival Studies, or Social Self-Defense. They should start in kindergarten.

Advertising

By the time the average North American child graduates from high school, he will have seen close to 700,000 commercials on TV. If you add billboards, radio, newspapers and magazines, you can safely assume one million pitches to "Buy! Buy! Buy!" before he gets to vote. No wonder the poor kid has trouble with his mind! If you were told at his birth that your child would be accosted by a million live salesmen before he grew up, all of them screaming "Hey, wanna be happy? Have I the thing for you!," wouldn't you be out there with a two-by-four (in Canada) or a shotgun (in the U.S.) shooing them away? Wouldn't you be writing letters to your congressman, the Pope and Oprah screaming your legitimate complaint? So why not treat the electronic and paper hucksters the same way? Why not give our children a course in advertising; *not* how to do it, but how to defend against it. Teach them what it is trying to do and how it does it. And teach them that it is a not-so-subtle form of brainwashing that, as NYU professor and media critic Neil Postman said, "Tells us that all our problems are solvable . . . through the purchase of some chemical, food, drug or machine." And the greatest threat of advertising is that once it teaches our children that they can have salvation if they buy, they silently accept that they *cannot* have salvation *unless* they do.

Comprehensive defense against advertising would protect their physical health as well by explaining to them that slogans like "You've come a long way, Baby," really mean you've come closer to the morgue to join the other 300,000 North Americans who die varied horrible deaths *each year* of smoking. But explaining advertising will do nothing unless you teach them about addictive habits, how and why they happen, how they can be avoided, and how to obtain help and happiness from people instead of possessions.

It will be a long course, Baby.

Nutrition, Chemistry and Cooking

Forty years ago we could have done without this. Most people bought pure, clean food, and actually had the mental vigor to cook up a simple meal. Now we open cans, packages, eat from stalls, troughs and take-outs, and what the hell we're eating, Heaven only knows. Disgusting. Worldwide there are some "70,000 chemicals currently in use with between 500 and 1,000 new ones being added every year." I'm not saying they're all right there in your hot pastrami, coleslaw and Diet Cola, but then again. . . . If we are about to slowly exterminate our children (the National Academy of Sciences estimates that pesticide in food may give this generation of Americans one million cases of cancer) should we not at least give them a fighting chance and arm them with some knowledge? Should we not teach them about preservatives, pesticides, and additives, before these kill them?

And we should teach them about nutrition, the foods they eat; which does them what good, which causes what harm. Teach them that Coke is not only "it" but that it also rots your teeth. Teach them that homemade lemonade is much better for them, costs a lot less, and causes a lot less pollution. Teach them that it takes fifteen pounds of grain and soybeans to produce one edible pound of beef, and seven pounds to produce a pound of pork. Explain to them that if a half-dozen of them switched from eating hamburgers and steak to more vegetables and grain, they could, among them, save fourteen acres of rainforest from being cut down for farmland and about 2,000 gallons of oil (and pesticides) it would take to grow fourteen acres of grain.

Livestock and Politicians

Then we should have a quick combined course in animal husbandry and government just so our kids could learn to distinguish good-for-the-garden bullshit from the other kind.

New-History

Given the devastation of our planet triggered by the greed and overconsumption of a relatively small number of ignorant, power-hungry "blobs", would it not make sense to teach our children not about demented kings and queens and princes of industry, and the grotesquely motivated pyramids and edifices they built in their own honor, but about the great gentle masses through the ages, the nameless, harmless humanity? Would it not make sense to teach our children how humble, simple people—the peasants, the craftsmen, the fishermen, the country doctor—managed to live through the centuries? They should be our heroes, for they have withstood endless misery at the hands of the well-remembered, with whose life stories we bore our children now.

Religious Studies

It is most curious that we leave the teachings of the kindest and wisest men of history to mostly ignored courses at universities. Would the wisdom of Buddha, Jesus, and Mohammed and the teachings of myriad native tribes, with their all-encompassing view of man, Nature, life, and the universe, not be an infinitely more sound foundation for our children than obscure details about which insecure, jingoistic runt defeated which rabid loony where?

It is this lack of an overview of life, this lack of an attempt to give an overall perspective to the relationship between man and man, man and the earth, man and history, that leads to a morally and philosophically hollow citizenry, led by men and women who are convinced that "A Philosophy of Life" is a long-running soap on the tube every morning.

Reasoning and Critical Thinking

In this age of information, few things could be more important to teach our children than to be analytical and critical about what they read and are told. We take pride that everyone has instant access to almost limitless information, and that's nice. But how little that information is analyzed and assimilated is frightening. We seem to have become not much more than regurgitators of factoids, which by themselves are not only of little value, but often do much harm. The harm comes in that they tend to encourage non-continuous thought, leaving us vulnerable to, and satisfied with, almost senseless slogans, to the point where our conversations, and indeed our thinking, become indistinguishable from the worst tabloid headlines. And what a chaotic mess that must cause in our brains! Almost limitless examples of this were uttered by the citizenry as they tried to endorse the Gulf War once it started. The most reassuring I heard was, "We elected him president so he must know what he's doing."

Facts have little to do with knowledge, yet facts about the most inutile trivia seem now to be the mania of our lives. A small newspaper store in mid-Manhattan carries 3,500 (no misprint) different magazines. Filled with how much truly enlightening stuff?

Just how badly we need to be critical and analytical about what we are fed is exemplified by the following. The tobacco industry has finally given up trying to deny that their product is the world's single most effective weapon against overpopulation. Their new lobby, or reasoning (and I quote from a CBC interview with the soft-voiced spokesman of the Canadian cigarette industry) is that "smoking is not only a question of health, but is also *a question of tax revenues and jobs.*" Oh, now I get it! What the old velvet-hummer was saying was that we need cigarette sales to: 1) get tax revenues to pay for the hospitalization of all those who got cancer from smoking, and 2) to provide jobs so people will be able to afford a nice funeral when they die from smoking.

Since it would probably take some time to establish an instant-response-by-guillotine to such mind-insulting bullshit, it would probably behoove us to begin crash courses in reasoning and critical thinking, to mentally vaccinate our children at an early, early age.

The Environment

It is safe to say that there is no greater current threat to our children than the destruction by their elders of the world around them. To give them a broad understanding of the results of all of our actions is essential. They need to understand that no human action lives in isolation; it has a result that, in some small way, can affect us all. And small things add up.

It is time for a Children's Bill of Rights. Every child born on this Earth has a God-given right to clean air, clean water, clean food, tranquility and unspoiled natural beauty. (And, on his birthday, all the rocky-road ice-cream he can eat.) Children should be taught that. Should be taught to demand it. Should be taught, if the need arises, to fight for it.

Along with their rights they should be taught a Bill of Responsibilities. As Solzhenitsyn so profoundly observed, "Western civilization has spent three hundred years demanding rights, with almost no mention of responsibilities." First responsibility: Think through completely what you plan to do. Second responsibility: Don't do it; there are too many people doing it already. You'll just end up making a mess and who'll clean up after you? You lived fine without it so far, so why bother? Have another beer.

Farming

Every child, by the time he leaves elementary school, should know first hand—*not from bloody video!*—how to grow his own food, raise chickens, and cook them, so that when this crack-a-joke, house-of-gadgets of a society crumbles, and the last investment banker lies dead of starvation in front of an empty deli, he can be happily whistling in the fields with his little hoe.

Building

And know how to build his own house out of wood, stone, sticks and mud.

Rollicking fun

No one in the world knows how to live life to the fullest as a child does. Whatever it takes to keep that spark alive, *whatever creativity, whatever effort on our part,* it should be done.

One last comment. There is a frightening movement under way to turn our adult-abandoned, machine-numbed, alienated-from-humanity-and-reality children into something even worse. A Mr. Christopher Whittle (he's the little chap who provides those lovely 12-minute kiddie-news TV programs free of charge to all our schools—provided that the teachers wedge the kids' eyes open with toothpicks so they can't *not* watch the commercials) wants to keep our children away from home and adult society for eleven months a year, from early morning until early evening, surrounded *not* by passionate, flesh-and-blood teachers, but by the latest technology. He wants to equip each child with a mechanical "learning partner"—a computer, monitor, printer, VCR, FAX machine, paintboard, stereo and telephone. All of them, we assume, belching nicely spaced commercials.

I would like to respectfully suggest a "learning partner" for our Mr. Whittle: A rocket ship. With him tied firmly to it and the controls locked for a one-way trip to Uranus.

❋

And a very last comment. It is futile to attempt to cure our educational system as if it existed in hermetic isolation. It is an inseparable part of our chaotic, ruthless world. And, as Lewis Mumford said, "Unless we challenge the current American way of life, all we can expect is more and more of worse and worse."

14

THE SELF-HELPLESS
SOCIETY

In a society as highly organized as Western culture, a person depends upon many other people and upon conditions in general for his security. This means, of course, that a person's security may often be threatened or lost through no fault of his own or without any opportunity to regain it. *For that reason, security takes on a special importance in people's lives—more so in many cases than other human motives—and it is responsible for much personal unhappiness as well as social unrest.*
   —Dr. Clifford T. Morgan and Richard A. King
   Introduction to Psychology

Strangely enough, insecurity, besides being promoted by our culture, is just as often nurtured by ourselves. It begins because we humans tend to mistake ourselves for complex creatures by our very nature, with an infinite number of drives, needs and desires. One of our fiercest battle cries in the war of the sexes is based on this very notion: "You don't understand me!" By this we seldom imply that *you* are irredeemably ill-equipped for the task, but rather that *I am* infinitely too complex for you to fathom. This, unfortunately, is Dream City. In truth we are as simple and predictable as cows. How else could anyone sell us ten trillion identical hamburgers, a jillion bottles of dark-brown sugar water, and an infinite deluge of indistinguishably inane TV shows and sports?

It is of course true that human behavior does become bewildering in some circumstances, but most of this is not due to "our very nature." Our very nature in point of fact is made up of a smallish batch of primary or un-learned drives: body-temperature maintenance, pain avoidance, thirst, hunger, sleep, the maternal drive, and sex. These, along with some general but still unlearned drives such as activity, fear, curiosity and affection round out the basic human infant.

So far so good because most of us can, with varying degrees of difficulty, satisfy the above. Our problems arise from the relentless emphasis on secondary or learned drives that *society* beats into us as we grow. A short list of these include affiliation with others, social approval, sta-tus, security, and achievement. You can tell by the flutter in your belly that we are treading here on more fragile ground. Others may glance at this list and say "satisfying these drives is no big deal" and in most mentally healthy societies it isn't. But all hell breaks loose when a culture puts disproportionate emphasis on some learned drives, throwing the balance of drives off kilter.

Just how negatively learned drives can affect our self-image, making us more insecure by the day as we grow older, is sadly demonstrated in the following study. In 1991 the American Association of University Women did a survey of 3,000 kids, asking them if they were happy with themselves the way they were. Of elementary-school-age white girls *only 55 percent* said they were happy with themselves. This is a tragedy. What horrors have we done as parents, as a society, what unattainable stupidities could we have set for them as ideals, that could make children, in what should be the most joyful, exuberant time of life, unhappy with who they are? If there really was a law against child abuse, we would all be rotting behind bars.

But that was the good news.

The bad news was that when high school girls were questioned, the percentage that said they were happy with themselves shriveled from the meager 55 percent to a catastrophic 22 percent. So whatever horrors we committed between the cradle and grade school, we gave to them in spades in the years that followed. The study doesn't say what happened after high school. But you have to wonder. Given the precipitousness of the fall between childhood and adolescence, it is hard not to ask yourself how close they get to zero by the time they are grown women. And all those women who think so little of themselves, what have they to offer to friends, or mates, or children?

Now in a decent society, one that put the well-being and happiness of its members at the forefront, every effort would be made to assure that learned drives had a positive effect on its people. Or, if that proved difficult, the society would make sure each member could satisfy his learned needs of status, achievement, etc. with the least possible emotional pain. To do this, the society could so reduce the social value of drives like status that satisfying them would be a cinch, or, if the society chose to give them high value (which is stupid), then it could provide ample means to their quick attainment so we could get on with more noble drives such as eating better, drinking better and having a lot more sex.

Unfortunately for us North Americans, the likelihood of society changing to fit either of these conditions is about the same as hell freezing over, for it would lead to an immediate collapse of the whole chase-money-and-glory-until-the-day-you-die fiasco which we, so optimistically and perhaps wistfully, call Life.

How so?

It is widely accepted that ours is a consumer-driven culture. What is much less talked about is "What drives the consumer to consume?" It seems we have created a society so harsh and complex that it makes us feel helpless and insecure; makes us long for improvement. But truly improving ourselves or our lot is a superhuman task, so we do what we can instead; we shop. The economy grows, the world gets more complex, we feel more helpless and insecure so we shop some more.

Any visit to a supermarket or mall will, after a quick scrutiny of the offered goods, make obvious that our economic system is based on our buying stuff we never dreamed of wanting, stuff no human being could *possibly* ever need.

Yet the whole consumer-propelled system is founded on the certainty that it *can* get us to let go of our senses long enough to shell out our hard-earned money on the most absurd bits of junk. The formula is simple and common knowledge in advertising. You create an ad that will make us feel ever so slightly inadequate, then offer a product to make us whole again. Bingo! With our omnipresent mass media we can be conned into buying even the most embarrassing crock of doo-doo within days. With our learned drives well ingrained, we are helpless victims, poised to fulfill perverse commands of the relatively few. If we could simply buy some product that was highly esteemed and be happy with it for life, things would work out fine. But that too would lead to economic collapse. So today's goal must become tomorrow's castoff, and billboards, TV, radio and magazines must keep pumping out daily new salvations. Bombarded by the trillion indispensables we need to make us whole, we are, by the time we reach puberty, reduced to the most neurotic, helpless mob that ever walked the planet.

Many will say buying a few things can't be all that harmful, makes you feel better when you're down and helps you pass the time. True, but therein lies the danger. First, the good feeling you get from shopping is the most shallow of emotions. Not only does it not help you solve the problem that made you feel down in the first place, it actually helps you hide it. And hidden problems never go away, they just add up. So often shopping just makes matters worse. A good example is the behavior of the daughter of a friend.

The parents divorced when the child was eight. She stayed with her mother. She interpreted the divorce as rejection by her father. On her visits with him, if she got depressed, instead of talking out the problem, he gave her a hundred dollars to go shopping and feel better. He meant well. Eventually she became obsessed with buying clothes. She now lives on her own and works as a waitress. She still sees clothes as her principal salvation. When she's depressed she shops. Then she realizes she's further in debt, she gets more depressed, and shops some more and gets more depressed again. A perpetual, accelerating cycle.

The second argument—that shopping helps pass the time—, while very true, is more dangerous yet. Shopping is an introverted activity aimed at trying to raise one's self-esteem by having others approve of our new possession. But every hour we spend buying junk and *thinking* about buying junk, is an hour lost from making ourselves truly more interesting, more well-rounded humans—warmer, wittier, more intelligent, more insightful, more caring—which would not only have a more profound effect on us, but leave a much more cherished impression on our friends.

Indeed it could be argued that shopping and, what's even worse, talking about shopping, not only halts mental and emotional development but actually helps atrophy what little we had, reducing us to the most numbing bores God ever created. Thus the whole thing backfires, for instead of achieving the long-term acceptance we originally sought, it virtually guarantees us the long-term isolation usually reserved for the most monumentally dull. And the saddest part is that, at this point, with our minds and spirits in a shambles, we misinterpret this rejection as a comment not on *us* but on the *stuff* we own. So we shop some more. We end up furred, bejeweled, Porsched, summer-homed and yachted, with the glaze of insecurity now frozen permanently in our eyes. And, still thinking we have fallen short, we continue buying, gobbling up the world.

As our life trickles away searching for things to buy, we forget all the things that aren't for sale—the seashore, the meadows, the mountains, the woods, where we can find some solitude, insight and peace. And we forget all about Ernie Flint, and Eddy Emanoff, and chipped bats. Meanwhile, our planet is slowly going to hell, as we mass-produce junk that has nothing to do with the comfort or companionship we need.

If our society burdened us with only the curse of chasing status and approval, the task of pulling ourselves out of the outhouse hole might not be so hard. But we're not that lucky. We're double-cursed. We have thrown in achievement. Again, Drs. Morgan and King: "In some cultures, particularly that of the middle-class of the United States, achievement is a powerful motive. This is the motive to accomplish something and to avoid failure. We are taught that in the land of opportunity everyone can succeed at something, whether it is making money, becoming a professional person, or going into politics, if only he works hard at it. And success is highly prized. Parents prod their children to make good in school, then go on to college and finally make good at some business or profession. The picture is very different in many other cultures and in non middle-class groups within ours. It is a pervasive motive in middle-class American youths and adults."

To condemn achievement might at first sound like treason. It has been after all one of the key words in the American dream. But when you couple it with the drive for status, you can perhaps see why we are in the mess we're in. And perhaps you can begin to understand why all those teen-age girls are so unhappy with who they are.

Our obsession with achievement has led to some of the most mind-boggling slogans since the invention of words. One that parents love to utter is "Grow up to be somebody." Is this a joke?! Am I not somebody now? Should I grow up and be somebody else? Who? Ronald McDonald? Atilla the Hun?

Then there was the other one, "Make something of yourself." Like what? An oak dining-room set? Cup and saucer? Skirt and sweater? What? Give me a clue! . . . . Jesus, Mom! What the hell is wrong with us the way we are?! I mean if slogans like those won't propel us at the speed of light down the road to schizophrenia, what will? No wonder we're so thrilled when we become MBAs and Mommy finally gives us an approving little nod.

It's not difficult to figure out who came up with the slogans; the same guy who came up with, "Man against Nature." Some lifeless, toad-skinned sonofabitch slouched in his dreary office who wants to condemn all humanity to a fate as bad as his. But what is more difficult to understand is how we all got duped into toeing the dreary line. I mean really, Mom, what do you want from us? Why should we become anything or achieve anything? We already are the most miraculous thing God ever came up with; we walk, talk, tell jokes, some of us even yodel. We even like each other if given half a chance. And we're easy to please. You can give us a rag doll and we'll be happy for the first few years, give us a ball and we'll run with it for the next, then give us someone as nice as you and we're set for life. Who needs the rest? Titles, career, power? Give it all to Toady; he needs it. It's all he's got. We have the bloody world. Why do you want us in the monkey suit? For your pride? For the picture on the mantle? As Mrs. Rooney cried out in a Beckett play long ago, "Christ, what a planet!"

And there is an even better slogan yet. "Contribute to society." Good God, there are more than enough people doing that already; 5 billion tons of crap a year in the air alone, never mind the mercury in the water, the PCBs in the soil. Isn't that enough? You want us to do more? There is a movement under way whereby it is said rich industrial countries will buy pollution rights from poor undeveloped ones so they won't chop down the rainforest, poison rivers, cause the world more pollution. Commendable. But why don't we start at home? Why don't we take all the achievement-obsessed weasels who value their lives so little that they go to power breakfasts at 5:30 each morning, and let *them* contribute to society? Let them burn, and tear and plunder. And let them *pay*. Let them pay a decent wage to those of us who like to sleep 'til nine, then hoe our garden or build our house, then slouch down to the beach to see what's up with the surf, or go down to the creek and do a little fishing. Let them pay *us* for saving the planet. Let them pay us for the license to burn and tear and plunder a little more.

And so loaded are our lives with slogans that what little self-identity we have is pushed aside. We put on our slogan-blaring T-shirt and figure we have made a declaration of Self. There was a sobering piece in the Whitney Museum's Biennial in 1989. It was titled *Tormented Self-Portrait* by Ashley Bickerton. It was no traditional portrait. It was a large featureless black box hanging on the wall. Made of black plastic. The lid was plexiglass. The only colors were in the forest of decals attached to the lid; Marlboro, Tylenol, Blue Rock water, TV Guide, Nike,

Citibank, US Sprint, Trojan. Down the sides were two long decals declaring "Season 87/88," suggesting that next year there would be new labels. Through the plexiglass lid you could see inside the box. It was empty.

✳

The helplessness we feel is reinforced and promoted not only by the undercurrent of social consent and the incessant hype to consume, but perhaps to an even greater and more dangerous extent by the incessant promotion of experts. They are not pushed in a simple way like products; rather they sneak up on us with subtle changes in the culture that leave us, more and more, standing helpless on the sidelines.

Not long ago, when the world was simpler and machines were simpler, we had a much greater sense of security and control. And rightly so. Things that were made by craftsmen either by hand or with the help of a machine were often easy to repair by hand with a bit of ingenuity and a bit of time. When a wooden windowframe cracked or split a seam, you glued it and you clamped it and it was as good as new. And you felt good. When your kid's toy broke or came apart or was damaged, you could glue it or rescrew it or bang out the dent, and not only was your kid happy but you were now his hero. When the car wouldn't start you pulled off the air filter and choked the carb or, at the extreme, pulled the plugs and cleaned them, and with greasy hands but proud heart you were on the way again. You could rewire a toaster, take the tubes from your ailing TV down to the drugstore to test them and replace them, and be more revered than Superman when it started up again.

In those days moms, too, performed miracles. They took a plain dead chicken and made golden brown juicy things from it that made your mouth water. From a handful of flour and boring apples they could make the world's greatest pie. They could make new clothes from old, sew on a doll's head, and tell you the greatest stories, without books or props, that the world has ever known. But things have changed.

If the aluminum window fails you've got to call an expert. If the kid's plastic toy comes apart, all you can do is throw it in the garbage. As for the cars with computerized bits and fuel injection, TVs with circuitboards . . . forget it.

Mom too has lost a lot of her glitter. The chicken comes from the Colonel hot and in a box, the pie you yourself can pull from the tinfoil in the freezer and heat it, clothes aren't clothes unless they have the right label, and the stories . . . well . . . they are told by the tube, without Mom's loving arms.

And with the rise of our affluence, we delegate more and more things to machines or to hired strangers. As we do so, we lose, one by one, those tiny social functions a family once shared: cleaning house, sewing clothes, working the garden, cutting each other's hair, washing dishes. They were small, sometimes annoying things but they gave us something to do together, to talk about together, even bitch about together, and common things to bitch about form one hell of a tie. But little by little we lose these small functions, and the bonds. And with the loss of each function we lose the spark of pride that came with having done it. They were tiny sparks, it's true, but tiny sparks can kindle a big flame. And what makes this loss even sadder is that those sparks of pride often had to do with the fulfillment of our simplest, most basic needs: We grew things, cooked things, fixed things, maintained *with our own two hands* our family and our home; the foundations of our lives. And this left us with the secure sense that if the world went awry, if problems befell us, we could set things right—that we could always fall back on ourselves.

I don't think any of this is sheer conjecture. A whole slew of programs such as Outward Bound, designed to build up self-esteem, are based on making the individual self-reliant, and teaching him to look after his own basic needs. Just as this sense can be built up by small experiences, so it can be lost by small deprivations.

Once we lose these anchors, lose these small controls, we begin to have doubts. Once we delegate to others, depend on others for our very lives, is it any wonder that we feel a little helpless? Feel that without a steady job we might not survive? Is it any wonder we're not sure who we are? How important and to whom? And is it any wonder that we'd like to be someone else, just in case that someone else has a better hold on life? And is it any wonder that if we can't be heroes to our children, that we try so hard to be heroes somewhere else? The only question is, "Who will remain to be heroes to them?"

It is no wonder then that the strength of the family is continually ebbing. Sure you work your heart out at some unseen place to pay the bills, but to your family those are abstract, distant things, that in their hearts do not have as much weight as the birdhouse they watched you make, or the doll you sewed together, or the story that you told on some dark and stormy night.

15

TELEVISION
Zeros as Heroes

Setting television loose on America was like carpet-bombing the continent with Valium . . . daily. And the effect devastated everybody and everything. No aspect of American life went untouched. Families, friendships, politics, religion, how we worked, what we ate, what we thought, were all permanently dulled.

Families that had once shared interests and concerns now at best shared the same TV set and at worst fled separately to their rooms to dissolve in front of their own set. Friendships and companionships were watered down or abandoned. Instead of real flesh-and-blood Ernie next door or the kid down the hall, our pals became little flashing lights: Lucy, then Mary, then the Hulk. Politics changed from the slick, underhanded, back-room deals of those crazed for power to the nightly public ravings of the more focused monomaniacs. Religion became a national embarrassment. From quiet contemplation and prayer in humble churches, it mutated into belligerent ranting on the Tube, accompanied by Cheesies-chomping and Coke-slurping from the couch.

The wonders of television—not just the advertising but the programs themselves—taught us how much better it is to open a package and slam it into the microwave, or go out and buy a ready-made junkburger, than to actually use our brains and imagination and create a meal on our own. And it taught us how much happier we would be if we munch some Crunchy-Wunchy-Chocolate-Farties out of the cutey-sweety fluorescent-pink box with a genuine-fake-mother-of-pearl keychain in it as a super-dooper-special-pooper once-in-a-lifetime prize, instead of eating something dull and uncool like a carrot.

And it changed the way we think about our work in a thousand subtle ways. It glorified and idolized every single-braincell occupation ever devised; from meaty men who kicked, hit, dribbled or drooled, to skinny women with incomprehensible expressions who changed clothes often and walked as if they had a broomstick up their ass. They all made millions, were famous (what possible joy that could bring to anyone is truly beyond me) lived in mansions (likewise) and were to be generally envied and emulated. Thus, if only by sheer exclusion, those doing honest, simple work of true value to others—the farmer, the craftsman, the fisherman, or the artists who lived a quiet, thoughtful life, were made into anachronisms.

And television made us love "the new"; the new sports season (same dull droolers), new TV season (same airheads, same moronic plots), new clothes, new cars, new gadgets, all of which was the same old garbage in different shapes and colors, and all of which taught us that anything old should be cast out and new things idolized and bought.

And most important of all, television taught us that our families and friends are uninformed and dull, and that our true joy and knowledge come from far away, deliverable only by the special anointed few. Simple thousand-year-old traditions like storytelling, singing, and even gossiping, that had brought people together and allowed them to learn from each other, to entertain each other, to form friendships and societies, fell by the wayside, replaced by the solitary, numbing, antisocial act of watching the bloody Tube. Meditation and conversation and even the wonderfully joyous human act of humming or singing to oneself was replaced by the constant background babble of the beast. In short, we learned to long for and turn to, not friends and family, but TV.

The New York-based Roper Organization did studies that show the frightening results. The single activity that Americans most look forward to each day is not human contact but watching television. Even during dinner, one-half of Americans do not converse with the family they haven't seen all day, but watch television instead. And in times of trouble we rely on the Tube to cure us; 35 percent of American men said they deal with depression not by talking to friends or family or trying to think through their problems, but by watching television.

Some insist that watching television with others is a social act. Compared to watching television by yourself, perhaps. But compared to talking and sharing feelings and ideas, compared to live, unrehearsed human companionship, sitting in adjoining chairs watching television is about as socially interactive as squatting in adjoining cubicles and dumping into the same sewer. I remember on various occasions having a great time talking and laughing in friends' houses when someone came up with the great idea of turning on the Tube to catch some favorite program. The conversation died, the sharing died, the faces all turned numb. You might as well have dropped a bomb in the room and blown us to the seven winds, our emotional distance had become so great.

Still others insist that television actually gives us a social foundation; something common to talk about. This is true but frightening. For just as the only thing that is worse than mindless shopping is talking about shopping, so the only thing more emotionally and intellectually deadening than watching the Tube is talking about the inanities we watch. And the bad part is not only that talking about *The Wheel of Misfortune* or *Floosey and Boosey* is deadening to soul and brain, but when we talk about these inanities, when we spend our time, thoughts and emotions on unknown distant clowns, we are stealing precious attention and care from our loved ones, or our should-be loved ones—our family and our friends. It is probably safe to say that the average TV watcher knows more about the love life of his favorite TV bimbo than he knows about his children's, and sadly enough, maybe even thinks about it more.

In the same way that we rob our loved ones by caring about fictional distant others, so we rob ourselves. Our emotions and our thoughts become fueled and guided not by our own true inner needs and wants, but by the bombardment of fictional ones from outside. We react emotionally less and less to events in our own lives, our own relationships, and more and more to the fictional lives of fictional people. Thus, when a secondhand emotion or thought trickles through us we actually fool ourselves into thinking "We have lived," when in fact, compared to the power of our own thought or real emotion, we have merely sensed the passing of a shadow. So we satisfy ourselves with living vicarious lives. Instead of having real friends, we have electronic ones. They are easier to keep and demand nothing of us.

The sad proof of this came from an expatriate English painter friend at dinner not long ago. He is in his thirties, witty, pleasant-looking, a fine artist, impeccable Cambridge education, speaks excellent Italian, yet he lamented about the loneliness of the Tuscan countryside, or more particularly about the difficulty of finding himself a wife. He had been living there for four years, fell in with the social circles, both local and expatriate, always invited to dinners, always circulating, but has remained alone. He told us about how depressed and tired he used to get over this, until he bought himself a television set. He now no longer feels so "compelled to look," for he can "stay home alone and yet not feel lonely."

This sums up the insidiousness of television. It acts as every other drug or opiate; it makes us believe something exists when it doesn't. It makes us feel less lonely by making us believe that the face made out of flickering dots is somehow our friend. Well, it isn't. It's worse than an enemy. If the need really arose, if you really needed someone to make a bowl of soup or wipe a fevered brow, to lend a hand or a shoulder to cry on, or someone to lie beside you and hold you in her arms, the enemy may— overcome by human compassion—turn into a friend or even a lover. But the heinous flickering dots will flicker on uncaring, whether you yearn, whether you cry, whether you die.

Every hour we spend watching those dots the farther we drift from the society of man, because every hour spent in their company is an hour we don't spend in the company of humans. And with every hour we passively stare, our wit slightly dulls, our mind slightly numbs, and our passion slightly wilts. And we become one irretrievable, precious hour older.

And not only do we entrust the tube with our momentary happiness, but we rely on it for our future. We rely on some team of dribblers or droolers to make us feel better through *their* victory. Then if our team loses we feel a sense of loss; all that hope and support gone to waste. And if they win we really lose, because although we might be momentarily cheered, our problems haven't changed, they've just been buried.

Paolucci best summed up the one-way relationship between life and the Tube. Three years ago soccer frenzy swept Italy. The World Cup was being played there and the home team had a chance to win. What could be greater? Every paper, every channel had nothing but the guys in shorts; the theme song blared from every window, Italian flags hung over every door. In the semifinals Italy was playing Argentina. I asked Paolucci if he would watch the game. He firmly said "No." I asked, a bit surprised, if he wasn't excited about his country's team. He looked a bit puzzled, then sad, then he opened his arms as if to take in his family, his house, his friends, his valley, and said, "What do *they* have to do with us?"

Apart from the social interactions and the real emotional life TV robs us of, the greatest damage it does is to our spirits and our minds. In its presence we become helpless receivers; the only mental activity is in deciding to change channels. We can affect nothing that happens, not even the pace at which it happens, and as if the programs weren't obvious enough, we are even given laugh tracks to tell us when to laugh.

Since there is no interaction, no discussion, no feedback, only the power of presentation, we grow to distrust our own opinions, subjugate our own instincts and convictions and actually fool ourselves into believing the most outrageous lies, like that the umpteenth tedious shuttle flight is a spectacular historic human event, or that George Bush actually gave a damn about anyone but himself.

This willingness to accept what we are told, this willingness to endow with importance the inane and the fake, and most important, our willingness to become inactive bystanders, watchers, does not end when we turn off the beast. It lingers. Like a bad meal. Just as our favorite stars linger in our minds, so does this subtle acceptance of the given. We accept that we are helpless, so we become helpless. We lose our natural ability to entertain others and ourselves—a feat most seals and monkeys do with ease—and turn to the Tube to save us. When enough of us are convinced—convince ourselves—that we are too dull for company, the vast entertainment industry is born. And when, through a lack of human contact, enough of us feel too inadequate to deal with each other, to settle problems face to face, then the vast legal industry is born.

And when we surrender the will to care about each other, to govern ourselves, a painfully ludicrous government is born that makes insane, distant judgments affecting our lives. And when enough of us convince ourselves that someone else knows better about how the world should work, what is right or wrong, what is to be thought, what is to be done, then we will be ripe for the next Hitler to come and lead us sheep into the abyss.

Some say that the effect of television is vastly overrated, while others say it has no influence on them at all. They watch it for distraction and no more. . . . That would be nice if it were true. We are, for better or worse, a malleable race. It takes us but a few days of living in the tranquil countryside, of being exposed to the gentleness of the meadows, woods and sky, before our pace slows, our tensions ease, and we find a calm in ourselves and in the world. Similarly, it takes but a few days of living in New York City, of being exposed to the onslaught of noise, commotion, aggressiveness and ugliness before we become agitated, fast-paced, aggressive and hardened. Similarly, it is beyond doubt that constant exposure to the endless stupidity of television—the dull repetition, the infantile plots, the cardboard people, the hype, the senseless violence, will turn us, in spite of ourselves, into, to borrow a phrase from Colin Turnbull, "A society of the numb."

Or as the *Washington Post* put it, "Television is the dominant force in conveying attitudes and values for the whole of society. Anyone who has ever watched television with a child knows firsthand how frighteningly influential the small screen can be in suggesting not only what to buy but also how to behave and speak and, indeed, what to think."

Many will say that not all programs are bad, and that may be true, but only as true as not all sheep are white. Don't misunderstand me. I am not blaming television for what it is. For what it is, it is absolutely perfect. But it is only one thing and nothing more—*electronic junk mail*. What *is* frightening is that it is electronic junk mail *disguised as a way of life*. It pretends to bring all things to all people, when it brings nothing but a million guys selling endless junk. But instead of using just the right pretty-colored paper or just the right cute picture—like good junk mail makers do—it uses just the right TV shows; shows that will put us and our children in the mood to buy.

Hence, to demand, as many well-intentioned people often do, *better quality* television programs—programs that are more intelligent, more cultural, more educational—is shockingly naive, for it is much like demanding that toilet-paper makers print Shakespeare's sonnets on the wrappers.

The fact that this uninterrupted stream of junk mail has been heaped upon us unquestioned for forty years is truly mind-boggling. It is mind-boggling because at the same time we have learned to deal forcefully with that singularly sad wretch, the door-to-door salesman. Without a blink of an eye we slam the door in his face, sic the dog on him, or in a rare humane moment turn off the lights and pretend we died. Yet at the same time we allow a thousand videotaped hucksters to trample our precious prime-lives into the bog of dumbness every night.

It is sad that we sold off our free time, our free thoughts, our time with family and friends, and even our solitude quite literally for a song, and maybe a dance, some jokes, but mostly fighting, car-crashes, and a lot of killing. Programs which, as Bobby Kennedy said, "glorify violence the better to sell goods to our children." That was twenty-five years ago. If he could only see them now!

That we are getting dumber by the minute there is no doubt. Almost half the kindergarten teachers surveyed in the Carnegie report said their kids were less ready to learn now than youngsters had been even five years ago. Our attention spans have dropped like lead balloons—the average "sound bite" or block of uninterrupted political speech fell from forty-two seconds in 1968 to fewer than ten seconds in 1988. Many of us have become culinary illiterates. We cannot follow even a simple recipe. The 1991 Department of Education statistics on young adults say that 80 percent of them cannot use bus timetables, 78 percent can't figure out a tip, and only one-half can locate information in a news story. If that is not enough proof of dumbness, then note that we now spend $20 billion a year on cosmetics and $33 billion on diets, and according to *Harper's* magazine, the number 1, 2, and 3 bestsellers in college bookstores are *Cosmopolitan, Glamour* and *Vogue*. . . . Case closed.

Just as we lost our body hair and the toe-gripping function when we no longer used them, so we can probably lose—evolve out of—our unused minds. Perhaps you can't blame television for it all, but when something is so omnipresent, when an average child watches it for twenty-five hours a week, then you have to admit it must have some effect. Even the mild-mannered, cool-headed Department of Education, not known to point fingers carelessly, in its National Assessment of Educational Progress report blames the low performance of schoolchildren on three things: poor teachers, uninvolved parents . . . and television.

Of course the report does not hypothesize as to how teachers had become ineffectual and parents uninvolved, but if television so adversely affects our children, it would be fair to assume that it adversely affects us all. Or as Mr. Davis, the New Hampshire farmer, so plainly put it, "Neighbors used to visit every night and talk. But those days are gone. The Tube killed people."

So, if you really do want a more intelligent, humane, truly social life, one that is guided by your own feelings and your own thoughts and not by those of deodorant salesmen and clowns, the solution is simple: open an upstairs window, haul up your TV set and *throw the heinous sonovabitch as far as your arms let you!* I know the mess will be a nightmare to clean up, but you will feel oh so much better for it! After a few days of barely controllable panic, you will not believe how much free time, what far-ranging thoughts—some utterly antisocial but very enjoyable—what interests, what great conversations, what a sense of calm, and even a more powerful sense of control you will feel. And you will be free! Free to lead your own life, not some life broken into neat half-hour segments, one minute breaks, weekly time slots and various seasons, but your own, of wonderfully varied lengths of time.

Of course the great cry will go up that after an exhausting eight-hour day and a two-hour commute, no one has any energy left to do anything but watch something dull. And while this is understandable and true, is it not also a fact that the duller we become through a dull and thoughtless life, the more willing we become to accept things as they are—exhausting and dull? And thus the less able we become to create a vital, vibrant life.

If this generation is so bad, what of the next? What kind of children and what kind of world will those create who know nothing but poor teachers, uninvolved parents, TV people, TV cows and TV love affairs? What kind of drone will be born from the coupling of She who thinks *Dallas* the ideal life, and He who thinks the *Brothers Karamazov* are a *World Wrestling* tag-team. And what about the children of the drones? What happens when *they* begin writing TV shows?

I know of no test that has compared children who watch TV with children who don't, maybe because there are so few of the latter that they wouldn't satisfy the parameters of testing. That is just as well, for how do you measure openness, warmth, imagination and good humor?

I have spent time with a few. I spent a long weekend with one, walking through snowy woods on a long hike at Thanksgiving, and for pure wit, charm, spark and insight into the workings of the world, I would not have traded his presence for the company of most adults I have known. He was twelve years old. It is true that he had gone to a good school and has wonderful parents, but it seemed to me it wasn't just what he had learned that made him special, but rather something buoyant, exuberant, and natural he hadn't lost. He watched no TV. His parents tried having one and limiting watching early on, but that didn't work so the TV got the boot. His eighteen-year-old sister spends her summers working with ecologists in Alaska.

Another child I know is much the same; nothing you can quantify, just some vibrant human spark, a joy of life, something in his eyes, his smile that says, "Glad to be alive." He has never been sedated by the Tube; he is still as wild and human as the day that he was born.

I don't think it takes much soul-searching to see how TV affects us—I know some people it simply puts to sleep—but in most of us it leaves a numb uncomfortable void, an unsatisfied sensation so we go back for more. We shouldn't. We should go upstairs and open the bloody window. . . . Then go and sue ourselves for the life we wasted.

16

A GOVERNMENT
OF THE $ BY THE $
FOR THE $
The Business State

*Ordinary people are increasingly aware that government
policy is shaped less by public needs or public opinion
than by political contributions. What big contributors
want they usually get. Mere voters hardly have a look
in. . . . Americans think the system is corrupt and they
are right.* —Anthony Lewis

Perhaps no other well-meaning idea, possessing at a simple level such wonderful potential, has been so badly
abused, or as cunningly used by those hungry for political or economic power, as that of democracy. It is often
defined as government by the people, but what no one
likes to talk about is exactly *which ones?* Nearly half of

Americans have now accepted it as a sham, and have tuned out governments, elections and politicians, and tuned in *All-Star Wrestling*, which is no less rigged or disgusting but at least the guys don't talk.

For those who still cling to reeds, let me give you a clear example of how the people never get anywhere near what they want. Let us look at the 1988 U.S. presidential election, when the rightful candidate was blatantly denied his clearcut victory. In that election about 24 percent of all eligible voters voted for Michael Dukakis, 28 percent for George Bush, but by far the largest portion, 47 percent, voted for the best man: Nobody. Half of all Americans as much as said, "Fold the show, send the bums home, rent the building to McDonalds, leave us the hell alone." To put it another way, 71 percent of all Americans, either by voting or abstaining, let it be known in no uncertain terms that they did *not* want Mr. Cigarette Boat in the White House. And yet. . . . See what I mean about warped democracy?

Now, the adamantly faithful may object, saying that those 47 percent who abstained could and should have exercised their rights and voted. I am arguing that they did. But the system has so badly mutated, has been so tightly constructed to give those who run the country a firm hold of the reins, that it counts only what it wants to count, hears only what it wants to hear. And it wants to hear only Democrat or Republican—the same old thing, that doesn't rock the boat. That a totally new approach to the world might exist and is worth listening to doesn't even enter anybody's mind. So half the adult population of the country, instead of being consulted on their wishes or asked what ails them, are simply written off by the system as bad apples, too ignorant and lazy to do their democratic duty. This is partially true, for if they took their rights to heart, they would have been at the White House with buckets, mops and brooms, sweeping the bums out and letting fresh air in.

In a recent *New York Times* essay Lawrence Wright quoted a new CBS poll that showed 85 percent of Americans surveyed thought "the country must undergo fundamental change." Where, I respectfully ask, is there place for *them* in this democratic system? Who can they turn to? Where can they cast a vote that will somehow initiate a fundamentally different world? Certainly not any candidate from the two major parties. They, through perhaps no fault of their own, but simply because of the very nature of the system, arrived where they are, funded, tutored, and nurtured by the system. Hence, they *are* the system. They are an integral part of the enormous political machinery and the Big Money coalition (which gave us Ross Perot) that not only, as Anthony Lewis said, literally buys into the government through huge political contributions, but also exercises tremendous pressure through the vast and ever-expanding lobby industry entrenched in Washington.

This is now made up of nearly two thousand inexhaustibly funded associations employing more than 40,000 persons. Exploring how their actions affect the workings of the country, Lowi and Ginsberg in *American Government: Freedom and Power*, defined lobbying as "an effort by outsiders to exert influence on Congress or government agencies by providing them with information . . . support, and even threats of retaliation." Everett C. Ladd discovered who these groups represent, by compiling all lobby registrations filed (by law) in the U.S. House of Representatives in the year 1989. Of the total, 75 percent were by Big Business, either through individual corporations like Phillips Petroleum and the Kellogg Company, or trade associations like the American Petroleum Institute and the Electronic Industries Association. In contrast, labor union lobbies made up one percent. In a country where, as Sylvia Nasar wrote, "The wealthiest 1 percent reaped more than half of the $2.5 trillion rise in total net worth during the 1980s," where almost 40 percent of the wealth is owned by the same 1 percent, it does not take a genius to figure out whose interest the 75 percent Big Business and Big Trade lobbies were serving. It might not be presumptuous to say that government is, as Jerry Brown said, "Bought and paid for."

It is this great two-headed monster of huge political machinery and big money (which are at times impossible to distinguish) whose existence, more than any other single thing, has helped to cripple democracy, to bring it to its knees. So where can those 85 percent of Americans—who, to my mind are ideally qualified to be called Freud's "civilization's discontents"—turn for a new beginning?

That we have arrived at such a desperate social and environmental state cannot be blamed on the idea of democracy, for it is one of man's most noble inventions. The problem lies in what it has been allowed to mutate to, how it has been used, or, more precisely, ignored. It has become, as have most great notions such as Communism and Christianity, little more than a slogan, in whose name we pillage, rape and plunder; sometimes each other, sometimes the world around us.

In other words, democracy, which was created to give men the right to control their own lives and help fend off the shackles that the greedy and power-hungry would put on them, has become just another noble cover under which the avaricious and rapacious now officially hide.

For those who need examples of exactly how Big Money manipulates our governments, let me cite a couple. Dr. Helen Caldicott wrote about the octopus-like tentacles of General Electric, which makes a lot more than just light bulbs. Indeed, GE is one of the largest builders of nuclear power plants and "one of the major nuclear weapons producers in the land, grossing $11 billion in nuclear warfare systems in the period 1984–86." The range of its commercial involvement is all-inclusive: from uranium mining to plutonium production to weapons design and manufacture, and even nuclear storage waste. In other words, they can, in a way of speaking, see a nuclear warhead through from the cradle to the grave. Some of their best-selling hardware components are incorporated in the MX missile, the Stealth bomber, the Star Wars system and, everyone's favorite, the Patriot missile, made by Raytheon, a GE company.

None of this is too extraordinary until you realize that for all these toys there is but *one customer—the U.S. Government*. Even that might be acceptable but for the fact that GE's board of directors and associates are David Jones, retired chairman of the Joint Chiefs of Staff, William French Smith, Reagan's Attorney General, Harold Brown and Robert McNamara, former Secretaries of Defense, and Alan Greenspan of the Federal Reserve Board.

In this context it is not impossible to imagine a GE biggie sauntering up to the Pentagon to visit old pals and buddies, and having a friendly chat. "Hi, hi. What's new? Howabout a few more missiles?" And of course the old pal says, "Oh sure. Hell's bells. Why not?" GE is not alone in having influential former government members on its staff. Lowi and Ginsberg cite a House Armed Services Committee survey of the post-military careers of retired armed forces officers above the rank of major and found that "More than 1,400 officers, including 261 at the rank of general or its equivalent in the Navy, had left the armed forces directly for employment by one of the hundred leading defense contractors." So day by day, missile by warhead, the arsenal grows, and so does the nation's debt.

But back to GE. "In addition," writes Dr. Helen Caldicott, "GE executives also belong to key business groups and think tanks that exert enormous influence on government policy. These include the Business Council, the Business Roundtable, and the Council on Foreign Relations. . . . [and] not least, GE executives belong to very influential Pentagon committees. For instance, one executive who held various positions in GE, in 1987 headed a presidential space commission that strongly recommended that NASA develop a space station, and in that same year GE was awarded an $800 million contract to work on it."

A coincidence, I'm sure.

An Anthony Lewis *New York Times* essay talks about another coincidence. There exists a special club called the Team 100. This is a group of big-moneyed individuals—Donald Trump and 248 others, sixty of them developers, who paid an initiation fee of at least $100,000 (hence the cute name) to the 1988 Bush-Quayle ticket. According to an investigation conducted by *Common Cause* magazine, these 249 have done stunningly well in Government favors. For example: A California real estate investor named William L. Davis ($176,540 initiation fee) "is part of a group planning an industrial park, Centerport, near

Denver." Near Centerport is a small airport that Mr. Davis wants to expand to embellish and service his new project. But airports cost tons of money so he turned to the Federal government for a *$35 million grant* for the field. So far no big thing. The strange thing is that at the same time Denver is building a huge new airport costing the Government hundreds of millions. You would think that in these financially troubled times the Government would watch its money like a hawk and not waste it financing nearby competition. But, "In March, Mr. Davis chaired a Bush-Quayle dinner that raised $1.2 million. Two weeks later the Federal Aviation Administration made a favorable ruling on his airport." Now as Anthony Lewis so generously says, "Cause and effect are hard to prove," but then as my friend Ernie Flint says, "COME ON!!"

There now seems to be a country of three distinct groups of people. The first, the Government, writes up Purchase Orders; the second, Big Business, writes up the Invoices; and the third, everyone else, works all his life to pay them.

Meanwhile, a part of the third group steadfastly believes that because it drags itself down to the polling booth now and then, that gives it a say in what goes on the Purchase Order and how big the Invoice. And some still believe in the Easter bunny.

The most discomforting thing about the power of big government and big business is that it has expanded to such gigantic proportions. It is true that we all need to feel some control over something; a little power is nice and spices up our lives. Henry Kissinger even defined power as the "ultimate aphrodisiac." But it's the magnitude of some men's power that threatens to be the death of us.

The problem with power, and similarly with wealth, is that it is infinite; in other words, you can never have it all. You may, if you're really desperate, pretend you control the world, but then some guy called Saddam calls you "Wimpy" and you feel all weak again. Then you have no choice but to send everyone but yourself over to show him how tough you are.

Wealth is much the same. One big New York developer called it "a kind of weenie wagging." (This means, I guess, that if you're not too proud of your weenie, you have to wag your wealth.) Anyway, just when you think you have the market cornered, some guy invents stronger rubber for underwear and catapults himself right over your head.

All this desperate search for power and wealth would of course be excusable and of no interest to a soul if those in pursuit of power were content with dominating, say, five wayward chickens, or those in pursuit of wealth were happy to count their gains in four-leaf clovers. But they are not. They want power and wealth measured in Three Mile Islands and Love Canals, and Mount Everests of toxic waste, asbestos mines, mercury mines; factories that produce Thalidomide, DDT, and CFCs, 50,000 nuclear warheads with tanks and trains and ships and planes and missiles to deliver them directly to your doorstep. I am not saying that they *set out* to accumulate such enormous quantities in either horrors or in dollars. But both our society and their own sickness (for the desperate need for power and wealth is simply an extreme form of a garden-variety neurosis) are structured in such a way that it is hard for them to stop. The sickness drives them on, and our society continuously and amply rewards them.

All seekers start small. When we are very young we search for affection, acceptance, and love, mostly from Mom and Dad. Those who get it go on to lead relatively calm lives. Those who don't keep frantically searching. But our society is not a fountain of either affection or love, and even acceptance often goes first to those who achieve. So the searcher quickly learns to take what he can get, and he learns to get it whatever way he can. The power-seeker might initially try to exert his influence over friends, but if he has none—as is often the case—then he controls groups, clubs, or associations . . . and he goes on. He doesn't necessarily *want to* continue onward to always bigger, always more, but since he is still unfulfilled (real love and affection having not been attained), he continues on the only way he knows. And the more he achieves the more he gets accepted. And with these crumbs of acceptance he tries to fill the great void that lack of love has left.

The gatherer of wealth is little different, except that unlike his twin, who has discovered power, he finds lifeless objects easier to control. And so both of them go through life addicted to their ways, trying endlessly and hopelessly to command, or buy, some love.

Then of course there is the social part to this personal disaster. How sadly it reflects on us as a society that we do not recognize at an early age the desperate needs of those likely to become power- or wealth-addicted. How sad that we can look after drug addicts and alcoholics, but let the power- and wealth-addicted struggle without treatment, on their own. Sad that we abandon them to wasting their precious lives in pursuit of things unneeded for their survival or joy—things that ultimately have nothing to do with what they're searching for. And how tragic for us all, that we allow, indeed encourage, those with such addictions, such neuroses, to lead our society and drag us all behind. And I don't use the phrase "drag behind" lightly. For since both wealth and power know no bounds (how can they—they'll never find a mother's love in the White House or on Wall Street even if they search until the day they die) they, like the black holes in the universe, devour the world around them.

It used to be that you could escape to a quiet village and live a normal life. But now the wealth of a few is so enormous that it is invading the rural silence. The most idyllic old villages like Woodstock, Vermont and Aspen, Colorado have been bought up by big money's never-resting reach, driving prices sky-high. This same big money, encouraged by generous tax write-offs, has gobbled up range and farmland, so there are fewer and fewer places to go to live a simple life.

It is one of the bitter ironies of our society that those who have destroyed the *most* on this planet through pollution or development are rewarded with such enormous sums that they can buy up for their private use the few unmassacred spots left.

The problem has not always been so rampant. In the early 1800s wealth was distributed more equitably, with the richest 1 percent owning only about 15 percent of the total. The reach of the average neurotic—and there must have been many fewer, because most of us lived a relatively comfortable country life, with large supportive families to succor those in distress—was fairly limited by snail-like transportation and almost unlimited distance. Of course neither of these limitations stopped the fully deranged, but it did keep the garden-variety type near his home. So he might have ranted and raved around his town until the blacksmith or some farmer got fed up, whacked him one, and calmed him down for a few years. But things have changed. We have progressed. We have supersonic transportation and lightning-fast communication (although, as Thoreau said, we might have precious little of value to communicate) that give every neurotic access to the world. With country life vanishing and families fading, we are nurturing more neurotics per womb than ever before in the history of man. And with no farmers and no smithy, there's no one left to whack them one and give us all a rest. So they're swamping us from all directions, in sizes that grow more colossal and more threatening every day.

What great political power they command everybody knows: Both Saddam Hussein and George Bush could with a few words ruin our day. If there were only a few of these types we might survive, but there are thousands of them on our continent alone, scurrying daily down the corridors of power, signing little notes that allow their friends to dam things, drill things, poison things, and kill things, clear-cut the planet and strip-mine the universe.

What doom economic power and wealth hold over us is somewhat more hidden but no less felt. The awesome reach of GE was one example. Another is the power of the media that decide everything we see, read and hear. As Dr. Caldicott observed, "Corporations who own the media are out to make money and to control the public through a perpetuation of ignorance." And what a success story that has been.

But the way media ownership is changing, or more precisely concentrating—like most of big business— gives one even more concern. She points out that during the 1980s the number of corporations that owned half the

US media dropped through mergers and takeovers from fifty to just twenty-three. And the future looks even more foreboding. The International Labor Organization, after a recent study, predicted that no more than *six* conglomerates would control the *world media* by the end of the decade. Hence, a handful of giant octopi, owned, one assumes, by distinctively unlikable people such as Rupert Murdoch and Robert Maxwell, will have the capacity to turn our minds to mush.

Now the skeptics say this is all gloom and doom; mergers are good, reduce overhead, lean and mean, and why would anybody try to keep us dumb?

The reply is simple. Media corporations are no longer only purveyors of *I Love Lucy*. They are highly diversified. For example: In 1986 GE bought RCA Corporation for six billion dollars plus change. NBC was included in the RCA package. Good for GE, you say. Well sort of. But as I mentioned before, GE also owns Raytheon, maker of the famous (or infamous) Patriot missile, nuclear generators, hundreds of weapons systems and the like. So the more fearful NBC can make us the more Patriot missiles we'll want Big Government to buy.

This specific connection between Big Media and Big Business was sensibly questioned by Dr. Caldicott. "It is surely fair to ask whether NBC could be impartial in its analysis and reporting of nuclear power stations, radiation accidents, demonstrations against nuclear weapons testing, their freeze, or even the Persian Gulf war. Impartiality appears impossible." Those who take refuge in unbiased non-commercial public radio and television should remind themselves every time they hear the jingle on these outlets about how GE "brings good things to light" that not far in the background, Big Business is listening.

And even if a media corporation isn't directly tied to weapons manufacture or nuclear reactor manufacture, or something similarly monstrous, we are still running the risk of having a very few untethered megalomaniacs— not only devout believers in, but the *very gods* of Big Business—influencing, and even warping, the picture of the world we receive.

The well-respected late British journalist Peter Jennings, who once worked for Rupert Murdoch, remarked that editorial freedom doesn't stand a chance against a "proprietorial or managerial ethos which is unfriendly to honest, fair and decent journalism." Then he added, "I had no cause for personal complaint against Murdoch, but I saw how good newspapers and once independent spirits wilted in his presence—or at 3,000 miles removed."

And as we grow more callous every day, the concentrated power of Politics and Big Business do the same. Their power grows like a tornado; the greater it gets, the more powerful it gets, so the greater it gets again. And while one can see a tornado's power and know from experience that it will pass, never before has there been such awesome power in the hands of so few of the most emotionally unpredictable. And how it will spend itself we can only guess.

Both the absurdity and the tragedy of our situation was summed up somewhat inadvertently by James David Barber, author of *The Presidential Character*. When he talked about thoroughly examining candidates for the presidency, he said, "This person will be in charge of our lives." Let us, he meant, fill the position carefully. Why, I ask, have such a position at all?

Why should *anybody* be allowed to be in charge of our lives? Why should anybody—or even a small group—be in charge of anybody's life? By what right? Why can't we be in charge of our own? And if you think that "in charge" is too strong a term, then think again. Think of who decides things in your daily life. Think of who decides where almost half of your earnings go and what gets done with it, and how much you pay for eggs, or for a mortgage, or what your child learns in school and what he doesn't, whether and where you'll have a job, doing what, tomorrow, and how much of which pesticide is allowable in your food, how much poison in your air, or toxins in your water, or whether it's all right to smoke cigarettes and die but a crime to toke a joint and have yourself a laugh, or when you'll be at war and when you'll be at peace; and what poor devil will be blown apart, where, in your name. If that is not "in charge," then I don't know what is.

Is it not ironic that all through our youth we yearn for independence, yearn to make our own decisions, to be our own masters, and then we go and trade the control of a loving parent for that of a few neurotics whom we don't even know?

And even more horrifying than having one person in charge of another's life is having one person—or a few— in charge of the life of us all. How could a world of reasonable people allow a situation like this to arise? Why do we let some poor confused monkeys play God over us? How can we tolerate a system in which the decision of a few, always power-hungry, often not too bright, who live in almost total isolation from the real world and real life: traffic jams, violent streets, layoffs, unpaid bills, homelessness and hunger; surrounded by a secure wall made of layers of yes-men; counselled by advisors chosen to least threaten their hold on power; men who with moods controlled by hormone levels, old neuroses, sleeping pills, senility or testy wives, can, with the stroke of a pen, darken the noonday sun with missiles or with toxins?

Why?

And if you say that it's written in the Constitution then perhaps it's time you put that noble document to rest. It was written in a simpler world by well-meaning men, written when the air was clean, the water pure, when man had dignity and honor, when he tilled the soil and gave thanks for the rain, and lived a simple life, long before he mutated to the hardened rapacious death-and-toxin-spewing barbarian he is today.

So it wasn't democracy that failed us, it was we who failed democracy. We created a world so awful that to call it a "rat race" should send every self-respecting rat running to his lawyer screaming, "Libel."

We need a major and fundamental change. We need to abandon this "big-daddy-over-us" newfound feudalism and become free men and women again, to whom a democratic constitution could actually apply. For, as Lewis Mumford said, "Democracy . . . begins and ends in communities small enough for their members to meet face to face. Without such units capable of independent and autonomous action, even the best-contrived central governments . . . become indifferent to criticism, resentful of correction, and in the end, all too often . . . dictatorial."

17

REASONABLE LIVES

It is not difficult to figure out what constitutes a reasonable life. You can, if you like pain, do it by elimination, by listing your daily activities and asking yourself "How does it feel?"

1. Being shocked awake from a deep sleep in mid-dream by a heartless gadget every morning. Answer: Torture.

2. Breaking Olympic records in the Career-Octathelon: rising, crawling, dumping, showering, shaving, clipping nose hairs, gray-suiting (or Nairing, spraying-hair-until-bullet-proof-helmet, clown-facing and dressing), chomping, slurping, cursing, and dashing to car. Answer: Humiliating.

3. Lurching, stopping, bumping, gridlocking while holding back caffeine rush so you don't tear off your car roof and serial-kill the first hundred people you find. Answer: Trying.

4. Being locked in office or factory with the boss hovering over you, smiling when you need to scream, nodding politely when you want to smash his nose flat with your forehead. Answer: Unbearable.

5. Lunching lumpy tepid mush with the combined fragrance of Pine-Scent and puppy chow. Answer: Don't remind me.

6. Repeating all of the above 10,000 times before you die. Answer: No way!

Or you can simply ask yourself what you would like to do if you could retire today. Most people would say, "Get a little house with a garden in the country or in a small town and live happily ever after."

So what are you waiting for? Why not sell the house, pack up the kids, kiss the boss goodbye and head for the hills?

For economic security, emotional calm, diversity of work, and living in complete harmony with nature, nothing can surpass the classic, mostly self-sufficient, country family. As John Berger said, "It is the only class of people with a built-in resistance to consumerism." And it also has a built-in resistance to unemployment, recessions, inflation, deflation, traffic jams, and crime. In other words, it is the only class with a built-in ability to tell the hectic, frantic world to drop dead! How can *anything* feel better than that?!

And the social strength of the self-sufficient family is even greater. There simply exists no tighter or more stable social unit than a country family and its neighbors, all of whom share the same problems, same hopes, same harvests and same droughts. After a lifetime of research in both psychology and anthropology, Carl Jung found the hamlet or village to be the ideal human habitation. So did Lewis Mumford, who spent the last decades of his life in upstate New York in his beloved hamlet of Amenia.

Eventually society will change—it will have to. It will realize that neither environmental salvation nor our social happiness lies in monstrous, impersonal cities, but out in the country in close contact with Nature, real neighbors and our real selves. But if we sit and wait for the sick behemoth of a world to awaken and change direction, we'll all die of old age before it turns its head. If you want to have a reasonable life you will have to go and find it for yourself. You won't have far to look.

Small towns in North America are dying—except for those that have become quaint shopping malls for the rich, and are already dead. Some of the others want to be revitalized so badly, welcome strangers with such open arms, that they even offer free housing for those who venture there. And as for good land, no place offers more than North America. Nor is there a broader choice of vegetation and climate anywhere.

I realize that most of you will recoil in mortal terror at the mere thought of having torn from you the wonders of the city—steady job, museums, operas, Dunkin' Donuts—but I assure you life goes on without them. And is better. Much more satisfying replacements await you in the country.

And if you're afraid to make a complete break right away, you can do what our friend, Fred Smith, did some years ago.

When he was forty-four years old, working in a gravel pit doing everything from driving machinery to repairing it, he decided that he had had enough. On a small island about an hour-and-a-half from the city of Victoria where he worked he got himself five acres. It was covered with evergreens, had a small gravel beach, and the view across Welcome Bay reached the end of the world. On weekends and on holidays he started to clear a spot for the house and a meadow for a handful of sheep, to supply lamb for meat and wool that his wife Vi would knit into sweaters. He stripped and cleaned the trees and stacked them to season. A year later he started his log house. He built some of the foundation with stones he had cleared from the fields. He notched and veed the logs with a chainsaw and, since they were small, he set them in place with the help of an A-frame and Vi. The cedar shakes for the roof he split from logs that drifted onto shore. The stones for the huge fireplace he hauled up from the beach. He had a small local sawmill cut some logs to planks which he used for flooring, doors, cabinets, and windows. Much of the furniture he made from tree limbs. Since they could only work on holidays and weekends, the completion took over four years. But don't forget, except for glass and nails, they made their own materials.

When he was forty-eight years old, Fred Smith quit his job. He had no pension. After paying twenty-seven years of unemployment insurance, he received one week's check. The explanation was that he was moving to an area where there were no jobs to be found. He was on his own. They moved into the log house. Vi said she'd try living in the boonies for a year. That was seventeen years ago. In those seventeen years they have left Welcome Bay for only a few days to visit family.

They live by their wits and the work of their own hands. They sell fruit and vegetables and eggs and chickens at the weekly farmers' market. Vi knits sweaters to order. Fred helps neighbors on occasion with everything from rock walls to repairing wooden boats. On a spit far from the house they built a tiny cabin to let out to summer tourists. Their expenses are few. They grow nearly everything they eat and preserve almost all the things they grow. They are absolutely independent and completely secure. And if I had to name the happiest man I know, Fred Smith would be it.

So. It can be done.

Your immediate fearful cry will be that you are by profession a computer RAM-byter microfries boot-chipper—and how in God's name can you survive in the country? Easy. Because long before you became any of the above obscenities, you were a perfectly normal human being to whom digging, hoeing, gathering and hammer-swinging come infinitely more naturally than does byting RAMs. And the best way to learn to do something is by doing it. You don't need a million magazines, books or videos to teach you; the best book on each subject will do. But you will need some clear thinking, imagination, and good old-fashioned common sense. If you're stuck, look around. Go visit and ask questions. It's a good way to meet the neighbors and people love to help. And the more you can learn from those around you, especially those who have lived and worked on the land and know the soil, know the seasons, the more confident and comfortable you will be.

But no matter how expert you become at self-sufficiency, you will not be able to grow bathroom taps or light bulbs. Hence the need for supplementary cash. The most important step is to ween yourself off the things that cost money. Your TV should stay where it belongs—in the factory in Japan. Not only won't you waste money buying it, but you also won't be tempted by the tons of gaudy rubble it tries to sell. Try to make some of the simple things you need. It's a lot more fun than shelling out money at a store, you'll feel a lot prouder of it, and you will probably never replace it because you're much too vain to throw out your precious handiwork.

There is no need to go to extremes. You need not try to make a watch from old car parts, nor eyeglasses from a pile of sand. But you can easily re-invent things that you now see only in old movies, like sewing on a button instead of throwing out the shirt, patching holes in clothes, or even sewing them from scratch, darning, knitting, toy-making, furniture-making, preserving fruit and vegetables, and, as a last resort, cooking.

The cash that you do need can be found both in small towns and in the country, although admittedly in smaller quantities than in the city, but, as I said, you will need much less. The most important thing to realize, especially for those who think the country has no jobs, is that there are a jillion jobs but not the kind that require eight hours a day until you die. So while there might be no room for an entire accountant, there will certainly be work for a tenth of one. And while a full-time notary or lawyer or mortician would starve, a fifth or a tenth of each would thrive. On Fred Smith's island, a desktop publisher drives the ambulance and is the local FAX man. In other words, specialists beware, but generalists who can combine, say, brain surgery with a little tree pruning and sausage-making will get on just fine.

The best part of having a wide range of jobs is not only that variety is the spice of life, but also that in variety lies security. If the demand for brain surgery diminishes, the demand for sausages might rise, and so on.

Apart from every job imaginable, the country is a hotbed of commerce, although it is rather different from the city's. An antique store, book store, gift shop or gallery might open only on weekends. Others, a couple of evenings a week when it's too dark to be outdoors. Or an antique store may also sell books and gifts and crutches and sharpen skates—then sell even *more* crutches. The rents are normally minimal—a book and antique store near Fred Smith pays $250 a month—so opportunities are open to all.

Then of course there is opportunity in the land. According to author and organic farmer Eliot Coleman, two-and-a-half acres can grow enough organic vegetables not only to feed the family handily, but also to provide a decent living. Or you can be more versatile, like the Smiths, and sell fruit and produce, eggs, chickens, herbs, and plants and flowers. Old-fashioned gathering can pay in the oddest ways. One friend makes $700 a day picking wild mushrooms in season; another dives for sea urchins, still another weaves furniture from branches, and still another picks wild asparagus and herbs, while one of our dearest friends, Nebbia, scours the hollows of Tuscany for truffles with two dogs. If you are more ambitious, you can raise modest quantities (unlike the giant fowl farms) of organic chickens, quail, ducks, or pheasants for markets or restaurants. You can have a trout pond. Or keep bees. If you have a steady outlet either in town or at a farmers' market, or there are tourists and neighbors passing by, you will be able to sell everything from preserves and home-baked goods to honey, quilts, and arts and crafts. The world is yearning for anything made by human hands.

The service industries in the countryside are booming more and more as city slaves have less and less time to tend their country holdings. Building, repairing, tinkering, or caretaking for even a few houses, or looking after grounds and gardens, or even horses, or being a handyman can pay for much of a self-sufficient person's simple needs. Then there is always tutoring; teaching everything from judo to ancient Greek; or, in California, founding a new religion.

There is one enterprise most of those involved in seem to enjoy—providing bed and breakfast for off-the-beaten-path tourists. Oddly enough, except for a few regions, this simple endeavor is as rare as hen's teeth in America, whereas in Europe it has been flourishing for decades. I cannot imagine England, Scotland or Ireland without it, and Italy, Hungary and Austria are close behind. It will satisfy even the most hungry for company, is very light work, and requires almost no investment to start up beyond a clean spare room, an inviting sign out front, and some hospitality. Some of the most successful offshoots in the bed-and-breakfast trade are farm holidays. As cities get larger and farms more mechanized, the small family farm, teeming with fresh fruits and vegetables and barnyard life, seems to fill a deep craving in many of those confined to cities during the year. This is an ideal arrangement for those who run a farm, for their guests often purchase farm goods to take home with them. Two of our friends in Tuscany who let out rooms in their old farmhouse sell their guests much of the wine, goat cheese, sausages, preserves, olive oil, baked goods and dried flowers they produce.

So there you have it. Just a few of a whole gamut of cash-raising possibilities to escape to. And while some of the endeavors will be no different from the city's, the pace, the duration, and the fact that you will most likely be working for yourself will make a world of difference.

Some people would object on a historical basis, saying that country life has been a dead-end in the past. While that may have been true forty years ago, it is no more. We have made great leaps in small equipment such as inexpensive motor-tillers, more hardy varieties of plants, good organic pest-control information, excellent soil conservation information, speedy transportation to market (and the tourist market coming to your door), and the ever-growing demand for tasty, healthy, unpesticided food. And even more important are the new portable jobs made possible by fax machines, computers, modems and general technology that provide today's country life with more potential and variety than was ever dreamed of in the past.

Next to financial fears, the thing that scares most people about leaving the city is leaving friends behind. So why not take them along? The best ones anyway. Those who now slave the hardest and grumble the wittiest will make first-class country neighbors. And if you can't find the ideal village or hamlet, you can do as the Abbotts and Keiths have done near Barrie, Ontario: start your own. Beverly Smith wrote about their community in *The Globe and Mail*, and about similar new hamlets that have mushroomed in Canada and Denmark.

Edwin Abbott was 69 years old when he his wife Vivian and their friends the Keiths decided five years ago to resurrect that most civilized of notions, the hamlet, to live where neighbors know and help each other. They found a ninety-four-acre piece of land, part marginal farmland, part woods, where they are now, along with seven other families, all friends, "sharing ownership of the land, gardens, orchards, a couple of old tractors and even a flock of thirty chickens . . . yet each owning an acre with a custom-built house where privacy is respected."

Common property ownership has the economic advantage of enabling the group to own a much larger piece of land than each individual could have afforded on his own. For not only did they bypass real estate agents' and developers' profits on what would have been eight smaller parcels, but they were also able to buy in an area that still had large tracts of land, where the price per acre was significantly less.

Common machinery ownership not only reduces the costs to each family to one-eighth of the equipment's price, but also eliminates the pollution that would be caused by the production of eight motor-tillers, eight lawn mowers, or eight tractors instead of one. Besides, if something goes wrong, it is a lot more fun to tinker and bitch communally than by yourself.

And yet the greatest rewards of sharing are the social gains. With the Barrie hamlet, each person designed and built his own house with the help of friends. Most of the houses were post-and-beam, requiring not only a large quantity of muscle at certain times, but also great attention to detail. The community provided both. They also helped each other with some monument-sized fireplaces, construction of a common pond that irrigates the gardens, serves as a swimming hole in summer and skating rink in winter, and they make maple syrup together, put up each other's overflow of guests, and as Vivian Abbott said, "We've all lived in each other's houses at one point or another." And decisions are made by general consensus. All this does not only make life incomparably easier, more comforting, more fun, but it also creates a truly democratic community where each member can learn and exercise listening, reasoning, compromising, following and leading, and giving opinions free vent. If that doesn't sound like an ideal atmosphere in which to raise children, live happily, and grow old actively, I don't know what does.

Some hamlets also work orchards and fields together. This makes good practical sense, for then the *one* best spot can be found to suit each crop instead of trying to find one per family. But more important, working together helps to strengthen the whole community. Few things bond people more than common labor and few things are more enjoyable than the multitude of small celebrations working the land together can bring. From planting, to the almost never-ending harvests, to maple sugaring, firewood gathering, each has its own little celebration, even if it's no more than a meal together or a few bottles of beer. And these will not be like festive events you have known, where you pay money to be with strangers and sit numbly while someone entertains you. These will be about your talent, your work, your own life, with friends who are just as much a part of it as you.

Then there are the hamlet's houses. The Barrie group, while each of their houses is different, paid particular attention to energy conservation. So one is built right into a hillside with much glazing on the side exposed to the sun, another is heated by an enormous fireplace that holds heat overnight, while the Abbotts' 1600-square-foot home, designed by Mr. Abbott, is heated largely by solar energy, enabling them, in a severe winter climate, to get by with but a single cord of wood.

While each house is built to suit the tastes and quirks of its owners—moderated by consensus—enabling ingenious use of materials like the Abbotts' use of logs from an 1805 farmhouse—the unique feature of most new hamlets is the clustering of houses. While the traditional concept would put each family somewhere inside its own, say, ten-acre parcel, the hamlets most often group all their houses on about an acre, to create a more intimate community and to leave the rest of the land wide open and free. Nor are the houses then aligned in antiseptic rows, but are laid out in circles or other clusters, shutting out streets and cars, and allowing for the reinvention of such highly social traditions as the village green or square, and the village pond, both of them marvelous places for the children to play freely and the community to gather casually, without the pressure and formality of planned get-togethers. Some of the Danish hamlets have built common indoor spaces in which to hold gatherings, share meals, and provide shared day-care. The focus on children starts early and is constant. They are regarded as vital members, even sharing in light chores like egg-gathering or plant-watering, to heighten their sense of contribution, responsibility, and belonging.

All this sounds almost too ideal. Why should it? Why should simple, secure, humane lives be restricted to the movies? And why should new hamlets such as these not become the most common future habitation instead of something unique to be marvelled at? The critics will say this is old stuff, no great discovery. But I would remind them of Proust's dictum: "The real voyage of discovery consists not in seeking new landscapes but in having new eyes."

There are dangers involved, to be sure; the site has to be chosen with care, the grouping of houses and their design are all-important, as is their construction, yet how the community will bloom depends on one thing only—the people. If they are gathered with forethought and honest evaluation, the community will thrive, as most of the Danish hamlets prove by having long lists of people waiting to get in. While there may be many factors you want to use in selecting your group, the most—if not the only—critical one is goodwill. Once it surfaces in a close-knit community, it will be cherished, rewarded and nurtured by all. Hamlets can become, as they were in the past, hothouses of goodwill and good sense.

It is true that the new hamlets are tiny, sheltering on the average thirty to fifty people, and small towns have only a few times more than that. Hence, no matter how fast they proliferate, it might take considerable time for them to profoundly affect society. But when we live in a world as devastated as ours, where we seem to pile one social and environmental disaster on another, then the small towns and new hamlets may be the first faint light of dawn at the end of a long and increasingly scary night.

So there you have it—a few things to escape to. Of course there are others; cabins in the woods, fishing boats, sailboats, and desert islands. But if you find the notion of immediately cutting city ties and heading for the hills far-fetched, too drastic, too irreversible, then at least do this: dump the TV set; cut up all credit cards, coupons, green stamps, crossword puzzles; cancel all subscriptions, prescriptions, addictions, memberships, affiliations, commitments and obligations, aerobics classes, kung fu classes, shrink appointments, hair appointments, and the ten-part doggy-dancing lessons you gave Fido for Christmas, and go home after work, just sit there in the dark, and try to figure out what this madness is all about. And what, if anything, it has to do with you. You might just come up with a better, more reasonable life.

18

A REASONABLE FUTURE

It is possible to lead a reasonable life in an unreasonable world. You can find a quiet village, or hamlet, or a small house on a bay, and live happily ever after . . . for a while. The difficulty is in keeping a quiet corner quiet for very long. The bulldozer of progress seems always over your shoulder, dragging behind it freeways, suburbs, theme parks, resorts, and malls. You can of course pull up stakes and move on once again, but how long before you run out of quiet corners? How long before the bulldozer has leveled and paved it all? Perhaps it's time to dig in our heels and say, "Enough!" Perhaps it is time for everyone to unite and turn this jerry-built wasteland that is becoming more socially and physically unliveable by the day, into a place where we can all live in reasonable calm.

The biggest hindrance to change is ourselves. And it is not necessarily who we are that holds us back, but rather what we own—and what we owe. Nobody is more flexible and adaptable than the person who has nothing, not even debt. He can turn left or right, lie down or run on, and his life, overall, will continue little changed. But let the average member of society change direction or lose stride and he will be out of a job, then lose the car, and not much later will be out of his house. It is no wonder that we want so desperately to keep going as we are, lest one false step lead to the collapse of our whole life-of-cards.

So the first step toward a reasonable world has to be freedom to change; people liberated from the prison of their junk. Once that happens, once our happiness and self-worth no longer depend on our mountain bike, cellular phone, haircut, car or yacht, then we can begin.

And we should begin at the very foundations of our human society. This should not be mistaken for the machine-centered, systems-driven one which we spend forever patching, with no wiser purpose than to fulfill the ever more abstract needs of our ever more gigantic and ever more meaningless institutions, but one that focuses relentlessly and unflinchingly on us simple humans. For while we might be dazzled by the potential of the latest gizmo we've created, our basic human needs, our basic human passions, our longings and our dreams have changed little, if at all, over the centuries. As Jung said, "The psyche is not only of today. It reaches back to prehistoric ages. Has man really changed in ten thousand years? Have stags changed their antlers in this short lapse of time?"

So we must send to hell the needs and wants of the defense industry, the oil industry, the banks, special interests, and even send to hell old General Motors, for in spite of the old saying, what is good for General Motors is *not* good for the country. What *is* good for the country is what is good for its people—each and every frightened, hopeful one of us.

And what is good for us is our own roof over our heads, a good meal on the table, pure air, soil and water all around, and a secure family and good friends, in a true community, to keep us company. Those are our basic needs. Their fulfillment must be society's first goal. Their guaranteed availability should be our sacred right.

We could start by recognizing what a treasure we lost when we forced the death of nearly self-sufficient towns, villages and family farms. And force the death we surely did, by focusing all our efforts and subsidies on big cities, big suburbs, big transportation, big industry, big business and even bigger government, all of them deadly to society and the environment, while we permitted the struggle and the death of unpolluting, humane country life. We called them victims of progress, when they were clearly victims of the greed of a few and the thoughtlessness of the rest.

Then we must make every effort to revitalize country life once again. The question should no longer be "How do we sustain the development of the Big?" but "How do we tear it down in an orderly fashion?" The simplest way would be to neglect and abandon them, exactly as we neglected and abandoned the Small. By placing all our attention, care and nurturing on the Small, all the Big would simply collapse. If the people in the country and the small towns were cared for and looked after, not through creating mindless jobs which teach people only sheepish repetition and utter dependence, not by building more polluting factories and megaprojects, thereby devastating finite natural resources, but by educating the people and giving them opportunities for true initiative, near self-sufficiency, and independence; by giving the country-dweller tax breaks and support of the same sort that urban millionaire developers routinely receive to build hideous skyscrapers, superdomes, and malls; by eliminating destructive subsidies that do their best to eradicate the small farmer who grows natural pure foods; by giving teachers at least as much respect and remuneration as we give the CEO of blow-up rubber dolls; the countryside would draw many people from unlivable cities and become America's pride and foundation once again.

Of course this would soon lead to small towns growing as rapidly and destructively as any city unless vision was used, greenbelts created, growth limits applied, and surrounding satellite hamlets planned—*in advance.*

New towns could be built on old deserted sites, or even on new ones. They should not be the random lifeless suburbs that we have so thoughtlessly created, but self-contained vital towns, based on Tapiola, Finland's human-centered town of forest and greenery. It was built with no other purpose than to provide its inhabitants a fulfilling place to work, live, and raise children.

Tapiola's town center has a plaza and a fountain where there was an old quarry. It is the cultural heart of a three-village community, holding a theater and concert hall, a library, an art gallery, a youth center, a pool, a gymnasium and a high school.

Its surrounding three villages—within pleasant walking distance—separated from the town and each other by parkland, are reached by peaceful walkways that cars and buses never cross. Each village of about five thousand, made up of town houses, apartments, and single family dwellings, has its own elementary school, small shops and a café, all laid out in what Tapiola's planners call 'perambulatory distances' meaning comfortable for a mother to push her baby in a stroller, to buy the family's daily milk, butter, vegetables, bread and fish.

An industrial center with varied non-polluting small plants is hidden in the woods. Here the central heating plant produces heat, hot water and electricity for every home. Seven out of ten townspeople walk to work. There is nothing garish or jerry-built about Tapiola. Wolf Von Eckhardt marvelled at the way "it seems to grow out of the rocks and trees . . . as though it had always been there."

Or for a less industrial version we can look to some of Italy's medieval mountain towns, whose inhabitants successfully lived together and cultivated the land in the valleys below. Some of these towns are still socially fulfilling and physically self-sufficient to an astounding degree. Most food—meat, vegetables, fruits, wine and cheeses—are locally made and grown; most professionals and tradesmen tend a vegetable garden, a vineyard, and some olive trees on the side; many things are still made by local craftsmen, from furniture and cabinetry to barrels, baskets, windows, tools and doors; much entertainment is local, festivals and theater largely featuring participants of each little town; and much of the travel is local—to nearby creeks and mountains and the local hot-spring spas.

The insistent objections from the unconvinced will of course be heard: "How will we pay for the infrastructure of new towns?" The quiet answer I humbly make is "The same way we paid to put the little tyrant back on Kuwait's throne." For if we could ask the Army Corps of Engineers to rebuild fountains and gold bathrooms so a despot could return from exile at the Hilton, then surely we can ask them to build some roads and aqueducts so their own countrymen can come home from exile in dying cities.

And if we can spend trillions on warheads, arms, and hurtling garbage into space, then surely we can come up with a few dollars per head to make every home in New-Town energy independent with wind generators, solar heat and solar cells. Research and development from playing Buck Rogers accomplished little more than to beam *American Gladiators live* to the mudbanks of the Congo and to give us a hundred new gadgets. Just think of the things we'll find if we put our hearts and dollars into developing independent, non-polluting, secure, and undepletable, local energy supplies.

But we will need to believe in the simple life again, not just in the kind cited by cunning politicians who throw catchwords like "family" and "morality" around with great passion while they sign bills to build more bombs, and to make their filthy rich friends even filthier, while a fifth of the nation lives a life that would make Dickens cry.

We will need to think like Heikki von Hertzen, whose simple beliefs and civilized tastes gave birth to Tapiola. He recounts how in 1952, as Finland was economically catching up to the west, "We asked ourselves, 'What are we to do with our new affluence? We can't eat more. There is a limit to the number of automobiles and gadgets we really need.' So I started to persuade my countrymen that we should build a suitable and beautiful environment

for everyone . . . that would be both socially and biologically correct."

Of course on our continent, where cars and gadgets are
still holier than The Grail, we have a long way to go. But
the beauty of this house of cards of a society we have built
is that with the commitment of just some of us, it can
quickly fold. A society that is based on superfluous consumption, driven more by boredom than by any human
need, is at the mercy of its bored and fickle shoppers,
who, as soon as they learn to entertain themselves, can
bring about an economic collapse overnight. This was
proven by the last two years' recession, when worrying
about the future relieved some of our boredom, so we
were less prone to amble around and spend aimlessly at
the mall.

If just one out of five of us with decent spending power
nailed our credit cards and checkbooks to the floor,
within months we would see a whole new world emerge,
with a new set of ideas and more reasonable goals.

After the collapse, a reasonable society would hope-
fully be born. Its main concern would be the happiness of
our children. It would do everything to provide them
with real parents, not stress-numbed, distracted, worn-
out commuters who appear now and then, and leave their
children's care to strangers and the flickering idiot-box
selling junk. It would try its best to provide parents who
were there when they were needed, with time and energy
to explain, and teach, and comfort.

It could continue by respecting itself and all its members, starting with the poor. It could rebuild its human
base, its vast human reserve, by abolishing humiliating
handouts for all, giving them instead the opportunity to
make a brand new start. And a brand new start does not

mean training them to wash cars or bag groceries all their lives, for that is just replacing one dead life with another. But give them true opportunity, and true independence, the kind our forefathers had, before 1 percent of us gathered up all the wealth. If we want to be a true democracy then let us give everyone something to start a life with. Even the most "let-them-eat-bonds" Wall Street broker could not disagree with that. Who in their right mind would start a game of Monopoly with 1 percent holding the wealth, the majority holding its breath, and the poorest 20 percent holding out empty hands . . . or a gun? What fun is that? For anyone?

So let us spread the goods. Let everyone start with a little basic something; a piece of this earth to call his own, a roof over his head, and the means to put nourishing, pure food on the table. A few acres of good land, the skill to work it, and a pile of bricks or lumber and the skill to turn it into a decent dwelling is the least we who have plundered the earth all these years should bequeath to anyone who chances to be born on it. And what a sense of independence, what a sense of pride would that give our youth, to help them start their lives. Whatever the cost of all of this may be, it would still not approach a $2,000-a-month welfare hotel room, or the $200,000 it costs to build a prison cell, or the $58,000 *a year* it takes to maintain a prisoner in it. And it would cost much less than the billions we spend on burglar alarms, security guards and a police force armed as if for war.

The terminally stupid would cry out that this is blatant communism. Hardly. In communism no one owns anything. This, instead, is perfect capitalism, where *everyone* owns something.

All we need is a few changes in inheritance laws, some laws to discourage non-resident landowners, and some land taxes that you pay in kind, and we would soon be awash in available good land. You could call it land reform. Anyway, it's a North American tradition. Our modern history started when we took someone's land and gave it to someone else. The pain to current landowners would hardly be felt. I realize Ted Turner and Jane Fonda are both serious farmers, but 300,000 acres (about 300 Central Parks) seems too much to hoe even for Jane. So why not have a yearly tax on land over a certain size (say above what a thousand Janes can hand-hoe in a day) of say 10 percent, payable in land. Soon we'd have enough land to give to every newborn babe, and ol' Jane would still have a few thousand acres on which to get her exercise. If she became distraught, we could always pay her with some blankets and some beads.

If the use of the land were intelligently thought out, with hamlets and towns that were both socially and biologically correct, think of what a vibrant place the country could become, and what a full life its inhabitants would have instead of the endless, hopeless squalor of the slums that only the raging fires of a wild rampage can cleanse. Almost half of those on the welfare rolls at any time spend more than ten years there, and the enormous number for whom welfare becomes a family tradition to be passed on from one hopelessly abandoned generation to the next is growing every day. At what enormous cost both in dollars and in human dignity! Would the world not change for the better for the neglected if they could bequeath their children a fertile piece of land, a house, skills, a tightly knit community, a sense of belonging, some self-respect and pride, instead of the keys to a tenement slum and the address of the local welfare office?

Once we have taken care of the chronic poor, maybe we can give a hand to the Fred Smiths of the world who ask for nothing, and want only to be left alone to lead an honorable, self-supporting, simple life. Maybe we should, based on the example of National Wildlife Refuges, create National Human Refuges, dedicated to the preservation of humanity at its social and environmental best. These could be the remaining most beautiful parts of every state and province, where people can live in peace without constant dread of developers or strip miners swarming over the hill. Because the Fred Smiths, by the way they live, using as little, ruining as little, and polluting as little as a human being can, have more than paid their social obligations. Let's leave them alone in paradise before we tax them all to hell. In other words, they should be rewarded for leading a socially and physically non-polluting life; they should be able to sell their allotted share, much as undeveloped, non-polluting nations plan to sell theirs to the overdeveloped world.

Anyway, in a reasonable world, the need for taxes would be greatly reduced, as would the need for governments that spend them. With small communities nearly self-reliant, or reliant only on neighbors, and everyone known by and dependent on those around him, our million fatuous laws could be sent to museum shelves. Reasonable, decent human conduct would be taught and enforced by all. We could once again become like the truly democratic corners of 1800s America, where, "Each citizen developed his civic mores informally, through conversations on street corners or in the square; in the day-to-day encounters in the shops; on the walks that took him past public buildings and houses of worship and settings of great natural beauty—that took him, if only for a moment, out of his private self."

What central governments remained would no longer be led by the belligerent, mentally limited, and emotionally callow of recent history, who attained their posts only through zeal for power, political conniving, and vicious public relations. They would be led by the truly wise, who have shown ability and deep concern for humanity through their lives. Candidates would not emerge after years of favor-gaining, kowtowing, and vulgar fund-raising, which gives those who promised Big Money the most, an advantage. They would be nominated by a Nobel-type committee, made up of the nation's most thoughtful citizens, who would base their decisions on a life of merit. The candidates could skip the year of numbing travel, posing, grinning, raving, glad-handing, posturing, and, as Bill Clinton said, "Learning nothing." They would instead, as we all had to do in school, write a simple, clear, easy-to-read essay (without the aid of speechwriters and hucksters) which, before being presented to the nation, would be examined by an esteemed, knowledgeable academy, judged for comprehension of problems and the feasibility of offered remedies. In other words, the academy would edit out the bullshit. This short and lucid essay, in point form if need be, conspicuously free of resonating moronities such as "It's morning in America" and "A thousand points of light," could then be presented to all, before election time. They could be discussed point by point, in family circles, on front porches, hamlet greens, shops, or village squares, without confounding advertising that, along with special interest and lobby groups, would be exiled to

Saint Helena. An oral test would make sure the candidates comprehend their duties. We would then no longer have photo-op celebrities as leaders but true public *servants*, whose concentrated efforts go to making our schools and hospitals as sacred as banks and malls, and to keeping our streets swept and the sewers flowing. No less and no more.

Cities would be livable again. Their population greatly reduced by the exodus to small towns, villages, hamlets and the land, they could reorganize into small livable villages themselves, where the car would be just an ugly memory, where mothers could safely push their babies' strollers to the local shops and parks; where the air would be as clean and quiet as in the country, where what manufacturing remained would produce everything with extreme thought and care, backed by an unconditional five-year guarantee, or better yet, one for a lifetime; where the city would be a center for the best a culture could offer, not a place for the richest and gaudiest to preen and strut their wares.

Mindless greed and vacuous wealth would die from lack of interest, just as soon as those obsessed by them were relegated from national idols to pitiable clowns. It can happen. It happened with cigarettes.

Some may say that all this is just a romantic's musings on a summer's day. I don't think so. There seem to me no great chasms between our machine-run, vulgar, mass-produced urban world and a thoughtful, humane, village-centered one. Indeed the major difference seems to be that in our urban world we confine ourselves to being performing monkeys in a zoo, just to house and feed ourselves, and to enable us on our measly holidays to rush out and pay for all the things we love: fishing, gardening, tinkering, visiting, crafting, woodworking, gathering and celebrating; all the things that in a reasonable village are the fundamental, sustaining, daily parts of life.

Then again maybe it is only a dream. Maybe it is only a wistful fancy like the clapboard houses, shaded streets, friendly cops and gnarled old gardens that we treasure in our hearts. But just because that America never was, must that mean that it can never be?

Epilogue

A NEW LIFE
IN TUSCANY

Outside our window the snow swirls down through the burnt-out buildings. We roast a goose. Wrap it in tin foil then in a plastic bag. The salad, dressed, we dump in a garbage bag. With warm dinner in arms, we leave. The wind howls full of snow. The streets are sheets of ice, but bits of frozen garbage stick out for footholds. At Avenue B and 2nd Street the pushers are roaring. Maybe thirty of them milling in the intersection, yelling, bidding with wholesalers, with walk-up buyers, with drive-up buyers. Cacophony. We weave our way through. Excuse me. Excuse me.

Yelling at a building on 2nd Street until Suta pokes his head out and throws down the key. We go up. Huge loft strewn with paintings. A big plywood table, piles of plates, a pile of forks and knives, a ripped-open package of cheese. Merry Christmas. The TV is on. Electronic image of a log burning. Pre-recorded. A loop. The same shadow, same flame every 10 seconds. "Gas!" Giovanna screams, "Gas!" and points at the screen. The electronic image is not of a real log burning. It's fake; something round engulfed by a gas flame. Yuletide USA. Gunshots.

237

Screaming. Heads out windows into snowstorm. A cop car careens around the corner onto sidewalk, takes out 50 feet of chain-link fence, skids, bangs, whines, flashes, then back on road and away. The pushers go back to yelling and screaming.

Three in the morning, retracing steps. Streets empty. Snow plenty and falling. White mounds like archeological monuments waiting to be excavated. A homeless guy in a wheelchair, mid-life, one wheel bent, pushes himself through the drifts. Snowplow screams by, blade down, smacks the mounds and they explode sky high and garbage cans and tuna cans, diapers, boxes, food-bits, bags, rags, stink-bits and a long red ribbon rain down from sky all over the wheelchair guy. He doesn't even blink. Pushes on. The city that never sleeps.

It's time to leave.

SEPTEMBER 1987, TUSCANY

We stepped out through the low stone archway, out of the gloom, into the autumn Tuscan sun. It was early afternoon, the shops were closed, the narrow flagstone streets deserted; Tuscany was eating.

Arm in arm, calmed by the warmth, the light, and the pitcher of red wine we had downed in a tiny *trattoria* with our lunch of pasta *con funghi* and roast lamb, we ambled in contented silence up the hill toward the piazza where the mosaic facade of the cathedral blazed in the sunlight like a million tightly packed shooting stars.

We were in heaven.

We had been shivering while researching a book in the stone-cold of Sweden, the ice-cold of Finland, the gray-cold of Germany, and the dank-cold of the French west coast, and in more than a month this was the first time we had been warm. We stared at the mosaics until glitter-blinded and wine-weakened, we went around to the small church garden, sat on a low stone wall, and like centuries of dreamers before us, gazed out over the countryside below.

A sea of hills rolled to the horizon. And on each hillside and in each dale lay a patchwork of small, randomly shaped, lovingly kept olive groves, vineyards, orchards, and pastures, a field of sunflowers here, a wheat field there, some corn, some hay, all odd sizes, all open and unfenced, none defined by measure but by streams or ridges, or the crook of a hill or fold of a hollow, with boundaries of poplars or a ditch or nothing. Here and there on knolls, sometimes not, old stone houses with their few cypresses, some fruit trees, and a carpet of vegetables. On a ridge, in woods, a monastery stood with a square steeple, and beyond it a tiny hamlet on a hilltop. And over it all the gentle light, the silence, and a calm.

But what was even more remarkable about those hills and valleys was, that even though man had, for millennia, drastically reshaped nature, every nook—ditched, terraced, plowed, gored—it had somehow remained looking "natural." It looked loved. And it dawned on me that all of this, the fields, the vineyards, the houses, the towns, had been laid out not by some developer passing through to the next enterprise, the next buck, but by the individuals who lived on them and worked on them and died on them and passed them down—full of pride—to their children. Things were small: to a human scale; to the measure of man. I was in love.

Candace was far away, her gaze fixed near the horizon. Her red hair glowed in the sinking sun. The air kept getting thicker with light.

After a while I said, "What say we move on?" I could not have chosen worse words.

"I'm sick of 'moving on,'" she said with quiet determination. "I've been 'moving on' with you since we met. Houseboats, sailboats, mountain shacks, that garage in Laguna Beach, the attic in Paris, the rat-hole in New York, the whatsit in the Bahamas. Twenty-two 'move-ons' in fifteen years. What do you think life is? A game of global hopscotch?"

The tolling of the bells rose from the monastery. Slow and sad, it drifted like a veil of melancholy over the silent hills.

"They're burying someone," Candace said softly, and looked as sad as if it were someone she had known. When the bells were still and their echo died away, the world remained respectfully silent. The sun fell. The air glittered with more light. After awhile, just below the town, rose the light sound of kindling being cut. Then a woman's voice, one accustomed to shouting, "Mario! Non troppo grosso! Per la Madonna!" Tuscany was waking up.

I laughed. "What did she say?" I asked Candace.

"She said she was sick and tired of moving on, and if she were to move on one more time, that's it, she's moving on her own, for good, and she'll leave him behind like camel dung in the desert."

Mario kept cutting.

"So you don't want to move on then."

"I just want to wake up in the same place twice. When I open my eyes I'd like to recognize the walls. When I open my door I'd like to recognize a face. I know this might sound foreign to you but I'd like to settle down. "The last words she articulated as if talking to the deaf. Her eyes blazed. Brighter than the mosaics. "You know I don't want much: a tiny house, some fruit trees, a veggie garden, a few chickens; day after day, year after year the same chickens."

Mario stopped chopping. The kindling must have been "Non troppo grosso" for no one gave him hell. Mario was toeing the line.

"Sounds good to me," I said. "But where?"

"Anywhere!"

She had said that loudly and it echoed from the church walls. An old man with a narrow-rimmed hat who had wandered into the church-yard turned and looked at us with as much open interest as if he understood a word.

"Fine," I said. "How about here." And spread an arm toward the valley below.

"Here?"

"Lots of room for chickens. And the people are wonderful—they actually sit around and talk to each other. They cook their own meals. Visit with neighbors. The country is beautiful; the food the best; art and architecture even better. Concerts in churches and castles. Great place to bring up a kid. I'll write, you paint. Even the weather is perfect. What more is there? We could get an old, abandoned farmhouse and fix it up. With a courtyard. Maybe a little tower, a bit of land, woods, a few rows of grapes, a wine cellar. Make our own wine. Old wood casks oozing that perfume. Chickens; pigeons swooping overhead. A rooster on the dunghill. Olives—can you imagine pressing our own olive oil, pouring it on a hunk of fire-toasted bread with a ton of garlic rubbed over it?"

"You're nuts,."

"Fine, a bit of garlic."

"What garlic? I mean about settling here."

"Why not? We could have a beautiful little farm right there." And I pointed just over Mario's head at a small farmhouse near whose crumbling walls a handful of white somethings grazed in the shade.

"A farm!? When were you last on a farm?"

"When I was ten. Summer vacation. I liked it."

"I don't think that qualifies you as an agronomist!"

"I'll learn."

"But you don't speak a word of Italian!"

"I'll take a course."

"But," she said flabbergasted, "you don't even know where you are!"

"I'll ask somebody!"

She stared at me in silence. So did the old man, his face aglow with anticipation. Hers softened with kindness. "You're a nice guy," she said like an attendant calming a mental patient. "But you and reality," and she shook her head. The old man seemed satisfied with that. He adjusted his hat, turned, and went.

The pulleys of the bells in the tower above us rumbled, the pins creaked, and with a great "whoosh" the enormous old bell swung out of the tower, the leather strap of its tongue slicing the air, swoosh, a wider swing, swoooshhh, then a deafening "DINNNGG" then another bell "DONNNGG," booming and thundering until the air shook and the earth shook, tolling for vespers. A short priest with large hands shuffled into the church through the side door. Then some older women came in ones and twos.

Candace got up. She seemed deep in thought. "You know," she said, "there are few things more horrifying than packing up your life and moving to a foreign country."

"Name one." I said.

Appendix

A REASONABLE
GARDEN

By Eliot Coleman and Barbara Damrosch

For most people, growing their own food is just a dream. We believe it is a possibility. There are ways to integrate food-growing into our lives that are simple, non-technological, time-efficient and, above all, pleasurable. What we need is a new approach, a reasonable garden.

We all lost out when food production became a complex industry rather than a simple process. The soul of the household was removed from our lives and put into the hands of "experts". Why? When a simple natural process becomes complicated, whether it is giving birth, growing food, or burying the dead, it is always because some industry is trying to sell us products or services for its own benefit—but not necessarily for ours. Somehow we get caught up in these arrangements to the point where we assume there is no way out.

Much has been said in recent years about the risks to our health posed by the way our food is grown. From the moment a seed is planted to the moment the fruit enters our bodies, our food comes in

242

contact with so many substances having known or suspected ill effects that we tend to give all of it a glance of mistrust. "Where has this cucumber been and what has been done to it?"

But most of the reasons for making food production a daily activity are positive ones. Participating in the progression of food from the garden to the kitchen to the table is an important part of the human experience. It involves us with the flavors and textures of foods so that we select the ones that give us the most nutritional value. Our own hand-dug potatoes or newly harvested peas are irresistible. Tasteless ones brought home in a plastic bag leave our palates unfulfilled, and we turn to sugary unwholesome fare by way of compensation.

If home-grown food is clearly better, why is store-bought food still the norm? Why not recover the simple joys of providing our own? When an obviously superior practice doesn't catch on it is usually because people perceive it to be more complicated and more onerous than the present one. Often a simple refinement of the idea is necessary to move from the contagious enthusiasm of a few passionate devotees to a practical reality for everyone. We believe that there are three mistaken assumptions that inhibit people from full participation in home food production. First, soil fertility is assumed to result only from very hard work or expensive soil amendments. Second, home gardening is assumed to be productive only in the summer. And third, food storage is assumed to require complicated equipment such as pressure canners and large, energy-consuming freezers.

A return to home food production requires more than a change of habits. It requires a rethinking of gardening methods. During the sixties and seventies there was a movement back to home gardening, but the way it was conceived kept the movement from achieving lasting success. People soon tired of the idea. Raised beds, double-dug halfway to China, seemed like punishment. Extending the growing season failed because the methods used were more technological than biological. Elaborate solar greenhouses were complicated solutions that required endless tinkering and close attention. If you chose to can and freeze you faced long days and nights getting ready for winter before the garden labor was even finished. It was a puritanical philosophy of life, that spoke of dedication not celebration.

Because it seemed to involve so much hard work and a great deal of land, home food production came to be regarded as an all-or-nothing proposition. It went along with chucking the whole system, returning to the farm, living outside the national economy, and making everything you needed at home. While there is much to be said for doing just that, it was not something many people embraced for long because it was so much more difficult than the norm. For behavior to change, the new idea must offer more reward than effort, and it must possess an elementary elegance in both conception and practice. An elegance, to quote Saint Exupery, which "had not been invented but simply discovered, had in the beginning been hidden by nature and in the end been found."

The elementary elegance lies in understanding gardening as a process, not as a goal. Growing food can be a comfortable, manageable part of your life, just as cooking is—something done a little at a time, as needed, not all at once in a series of overwhelming chores. Instead of the usual sequence—"putting in the garden", "bringing in the harvest", and "putting up food"—wouldn't it be better to have a garden that is "in" all the time, and a harvest that goes on all year, whenever fresh food is needed for a meal?

This sounds like something that would only be possible in a frost-free climate, or with a heated greenhouse, neither of which is available to the average person. But in fact it is easy to do without moving to the tropics or spending a lot of money. We eat fresh food out of our Maine garden every day of the year without a heated greenhouse, in a climate where the frost-free season lasts only three and a half months and winter temperatures can drop to minus 20F. How? By appreciating the unique abilities of various crops to do their best in their respective seasons; by growing them in a logically planned succession; and by respecting and working with the natural world. There are four components of the system: compost, cold frames, cool-season vegetables, and a root cellar.

Compost is the principal input that keeps a garden producing bounteously. You make compost in your backyard by layering organic materials to encourage air and moisture to permeate them. This allows the natural populations of bacteria, fungi, earthworms and other creatures to create the dark, crumbly humus that bespeaks soil fertility. Since the ingredients for your compost heap are either kitchen and garden wastes—carrot tops, outer cabbage leaves, apple cores, eggshells—or plants that grow in your backyard—weeds, old grass, leaves and stems—this wonderful product is both home produced and free. For extra compost ingredients you can easily replant lawn areas to high-yielding forage crops such as alfalfa and mow them periodically.

John Updike, in a poem about compost, noted that "all process is reprocessing"—a nice metaphor for this conception of the home garden as a cyclical process rather than a linear, goal-oriented chore. Compost keeps your garden going the same way the natural world keeps itself powered—by recycling organic matter. That's why it is so simple and successful. You spread compost on the surface of the soil and mix it in shallowly with a cultivator. No digging required. Plants grown in a soil amended with compost are not stressed for nutrients and are consequently healthier and more resistant to pests. Once you try using compost you will never want to be without it. Good compost takes a year to mature. The trick is to simply start the process and keep it going. "Making compost" is not a job; it is the remains of one season becoming the fuel for the next.

A *cold frame* is a low box covered with glass that sits on the soil. The sides of the box can be boards, logs, straw bales or concrete blocks. The glass covers on top are usually recycled storm windows. The size is any dimension that the available materials will cover. For taller crops, you make taller frames. The simple cold frame, which has been around in one form or another for centuries, is the home for your winter garden.

The protection of a cold frame tempers the winter climate. It takes the harsh edge off the extremes of the cold, the wet, and especially the wind. That slight moderation allows a wide range of cool-weather crops to be harvestable through the winter in all parts of the United States. In far northern climates where the winters are severe, in order to harvest the full range of crops even during the coldest parts of midwinter you may want to place some of your frames inside another layer of protection, such as a simple, unheated, lean-to glass greenhouse. The key is to provide enough protection to prevent the soil in the frames from more than superficial freezing. Each layer of protection is like moving the garden a zone and a half to the south.

Cool-season vegetables are the cold-weather equivalents of the conventional summer garden vegetables. Some 20 crops—both familiar ones such as spinach, leeks, kale, chard, carrots, broccoli, scallions, parsley and Brussels sprouts, and the less familiar like mache, claytonia, arugula, mizuna, dandelion, kohlrabi, chicory, cress, sorrel, escarole, endive and radicchio—thrive in the cold of winter with a little protection. These are hardy plants and are not harmed by freezing on cold nights. During the day even weak sunshine will raise the cold frame temperature above freezing so you can harvest fresh foods for both salads and main courses. Cool-season vegetables supply you with six months of fresh food with almost no care, no pests and no weeds.

Planting a little at a time makes the process of the garden continuous. After the various summer crops are harvested, winter crops are sown in succession. Most of their growing is done by late fall and, with roots in the soil, they remain fresh all winter. Many of these cool-season vegetables have become fashionable of late and appear on upscale restaurant menus. But in Europe, thanks to slightly more temperate winters, they have been traditional fare for centuries. They are not thought of as a substitute for summer foods but as a full palette of delicious ingredients in their own right.

The *root cellar* is a hole in the ground in which you store root crops over the winter when they can no longer remain in the garden. Whether as substantial as the concrete cellars of colder climates or as modest as the buried barrels used where winters are less hard, root cellars take advantage of the natural coolness, dampness and darkness of the earth. Cool and damp and dark are the ideal storage conditions for potatoes, carrots, beets, rutabagas, cabbage, celeriac and parsley root. Onions and squash prefer cool and dry conditions and can be stored in the attic or an unheated room. Drying is the best storage method for a winter-long supply of tomatoes.

A root cellar is an extension of nature's own system, since it contains crops that are designed to be stored underground. It needs to be sufficiently below ground so the contents won't freeze, but beyond that it operates almost automatically. As the weather cools down in the fall the earth cools, and so does the cellar. The high-moisture conditions required for optimum storage are supplied naturally under the ground. The darkness prevents sprouting in storage and keeps potatoes from greening. The crops in our root cellar keep dependably into June every year. By the time the earth and the cellar become warm in early summer everything is fresh from the garden once again.

When many people think of "extending the growing season", they think of prolonging summer and summer crops. Such a goal can only lead in the direction of high-tech, high-energy systems. In this garden we are only "extending the harvest season" for those crops that don't mind cold. For every season there is a vegetable—corn, tomatoes, eggplant, and beans in the summer; spinach and peas in spring and fall; mache and chicory in winter. Preparing meals in harmony with the climate is a delight. Don't we get excited when, in a foreign country, we encounter an item on a restaurant menu that has just come into season locally, and is being offered fresh, cooked in a special regional way? The cuisines of the world were developed around seasons and regions. Our own lowest-common-denominator food system, based on nationwide, year-round sameness, leads to cooking that is boring and predictable. Eating seasonally keeps us connected with the natural world. We associate young dandelion greens with fragrant spring mornings, fiery chili with peppers turning scarlet in the sun, apple crisp with the bracing bite of autumn, hardy leeks with a robust soup simmering on the stove when you come in from a snowy walk. Just as it's easier to write a sonnet than free verse, it's easier to cook well with seasonal limitations: they are a spur to creativity.

But doesn't gardening year-round mean a lot of work? Actually it is less work than trying to do it all in the summer. The trick is to garden little and often. Think of your garden as a patchwork quilt of different crops. You plant seeds in one small patch today and another next week. There is never a disaster when a planting fails, because there is always next week's planting, or next season's. Even thinning a row of greens becomes part of the ongoing process of gardening and eating: by consuming each week's thinnings you put food on the table at the same time you are giving next month's dinner more room to grow. And winter is still a resting time for the gardener: the crops in your frames were planted in late summer and fall, and sit there all winter—fresh, flavorful and waiting to be harvested.

Seasonal successions also mean you can grow a huge variety of crops in a much smaller space than that occupied by the traditional summer garden that grows everything at once. Thus they're a perfect solution for the town or suburban gardener with the use of a tiny yard or community plot. Even in climates with the shortest season, a garden 30 feet square will easily feed one person all their vegetables for one year. 30 feet square is smaller than the singles area on one side of a tennis court. The chart on page 000 will give you some idea of the sequence of availability of different vegetables in a four-season garden.

If you have more space and time you may want to try raising livestock as well. A couple of backyard ducks are a much better egg source than chickens. They lay more, do well on homegrown food and simple housing, and they don't hide their eggs. They also don't scratch up the garden soil, and will eagerly patrol the yard looking for slugs. A backyard milk goat or small cow will provide fresh dairy products. Enough in fact that you may choose to share the produce and the care of the animal with a neighbor. But for the average homeowner with a regular job, raising animals is often too much of a commitment, and the answer lies in seeking out local farmers who produce animal products in a way that is humane for the animals and healthy for the consumer.

Fruits are also a home garden product, and definitely worth the effort. Small fruit trees or berry bushes can be planted as a windbreak on the north and west sides of the garden. A bed of strawberries can be included in the garden, with a new bed set out from healthy runners every year. Apples, over most of the country, are the easiest tree fruit to grow, and they store well in the root cellar. Grapes, raspberries, blackberries and high-bush blueberries are the most dependable small fruit. Blueberries can be dried like grapes to make a "blueberry raisin", which lends a heavenly flavor to winter dishes.

Don't try to remake the whole world all at once in your backyard. Just start growing some food for your table in a way that makes it central to your everyday life. Once you begin to enjoy the food, the process will achieve a flow of its own. (Eliot's book *The Four Season Harvest* gives a detailed program for how to do it.) Too often gardening is like the great summer vacation trip that has to make up for 50 weeks in the city. Make gardening ordinary, daily, a nourishing interaction with the natural world around you.

Organic Pest and Disease Control

Organic gardening means less work, not more. That applies especially to dealing with insect and disease problems. The aim of organic gardening is to understand, nurture, and enhance the systems of the natural world in order to produce food for human consumption. Pests have a positive role to play in those natural systems. Thus, spending long hours picking off bugs is no more of an answer than using pesticides. The same goes for garlic, spray, red pepper, herbal concoctions, or rotenone. All techniques that aim to forceably remove insects, whether using chemical or organic methods, are counterproductive. They are all palliatives. The word palliative, from the Latin *pallium*, a cloak, defines any method that treats the symptoms of a problem without curing it. From a common sense point of view the gardener who avoids toxic chemicals is to be praised. However, from the point of view of biological systems, the gardener who uses natural insecticides is no wiser than his chemical counterpart—different ingredients but the same mistake.

Insects and disease are not the problem. They are the symptoms of plant stress. Their presence is a visible exterior indication that all is not well with the plant. No one would be so simple as to think that a child's chicken pox could be cured by scraping off the spots—the visible, exterior symptoms. Similarly, removing insects from a plant does not cure the problem or eliminate the cause. All that insect removal accomplishes is to pretend the problem doesn't exist.

The goal in organic gardening is to eliminate the cause of insects and disease rather than just treat the symptoms. When you begin to think in those terms a whole new world opens up. The plant bothered by pests need no longer be a cause for dismay. The plant can now be looked upon as your co-worker. It is communicating with you. It is saying that growing conditions are not conducive to its physiological well-being and that if the plants are to be healthier next year the growing conditions must be improved.

The idea of learning from your plants that something is amiss is nothing new. Any textbook on mineral deficiency in plants will contain pictures of the symptoms exhibited by plants in response to various deficiencies in the soil. A common example that many home gardeners have probably noted is the yellowing of corn leaves when insufficient nitrogen is available. The attack of insects and disease is just as certain an indication of unbalanced health as yellowed leaves. The remedy is the same: improve the growing conditions. To accomplish that goal you must determine what conditions are lacking for optimum plant vitality in your garden and then attempt to achieve them.

Take your lawn for example. Say you have a lawn that is growing a crop of crab grass, plantain, and other weeds but few of the finer grasses that you would prefer. There are two courses of action. For one you could purchase all the heavily advertised nostrums, herbicides, fertilizers, and stimulants to try and suppress the weed competition and allow the finer grasses to struggle ahead. Conversely you could study the optimum growing conditions for the grasses and then by adding compost, rock powders, peat moss, manure, aerating, draining, irrigating, letting in more sun, or whatever seemed indicated, you could create conditions under which the finer grasses will out-compete the competition. The advantage is that whereas the nostrums have to be resorted to frequently, the growing condition improvements are more permanent. If you doubt this approach, look closely at wild vegetation. Certain groups and types of plants grow successfully in one area but not another because the conditions favor them. You want to create conditions in your garden that favor vegetables.

How do you determine the optimum conditions for the plants you wish to grow? A little detective work is in order. Closely observe the plants, the insects, the diseases, and every aspect of the garden. Are all plants affected equally or are those at one end of the row or in the rows along one edge not showing symptoms? What is the difference in the soil in those areas? Is that where you limed or didn't lime because you ran out? Did you compost that area with compost from a different heap? What was different about that heap? Is the good section of the garden where all the maple leaves blew in? Or where the corner of the old barn foundation was? Is it the new disease-resistant variety that is doing so well? Do you always grow the same crop in the same place every year?

If you can find no specific clues to follow, try a general approach to plant habitat improvement for next year. A crop rotation will always help. You might grow deep-rooting green fertilizers, add different types of organic matter such as seaweed to your compost heap, and supply adequate quantities of rock powders for minerals. Think about aerating the soil with a garden fork to break up soil compaction or removing the branch of a tree to let in more sunlight. Evaluate all the possibilities and then organize your responses.

Palliatives are a deceptive trap. Removing the symptoms may seem to improve the situation but it is only a cosmetic improvement. Since it doesn't solve the problem you have to do it over and over again. Whereas momentary reliance on palliative treatments is understandable, they should never form the basis of your gardening practices. Creating optimum growing conditions is the one constructive approach in a dependable long-range philosophy of gardening.

•

Barbara Damrosch is the author of The Garden Primer *and was a regular contributor to PBS's* The Victory Garden.

Eliot Coleman is the author of The New Organic Grower *and* The Four Season Harvest. *He has been the Executive Director of the International Federation of Organic Agriculture Movements and an advisor to the U.S. Department of Agriculture.*

SEASONAL AVAILABILITY OF FRESH GARDEN VEGETABLES

FRESH ▢   STORED ▣

VEGETABLE	SPRING Mar 21–Jun 21	SUMMER Jun 21–Sep 21	FALL Sep 21–Dec 21	WINTER Dec 21–Mar 21
Artichoke				
Arugula				
Asparagus				
Bean				
Beet				
Broccoli				
Brussels				
Cabbage				
Carrot				
Cauliflower				
Celeriac				
Celery				
Chard				
Chicory, grn.				
Chicory, wit.				
Chin. Cab.				
Claytonia				
Corn				
Cucumber				
Dandelion				
Eggplant				
Endive				
Escarole				
Garlic				
Kale				
Kohlrabi				
Leek				
Lettuce				
Mache				
Melon				
Mizuna				
Mustard				
Onion, bulb				
Onion, green				
Parsley				
Parsley Root				
Parsnip				
Peas				
Pepper				
Potato				
Pumpkin				
Radicchio				
Radish				
Rutabaga				
Sorrel				
Spinach				
Squash, sum.				
Squash, winter				
Tomato				
Turnip				

NOTES

PREFACE

xi.   Lewis Mumford, *The Urban Prospect* (New York: Harcourt, Brace and World, 1968)

xi.   "mad, senseless . . .": Colin M. Turnbull, *The Mountain People* (New York: Touchstone Books, 1972)

xii.   Ibid.

CHAPTER 1

2.   Pollution by country: Lester Brown et al., *State of the World 1990: A Worldwatch Institute Report* (New York: W. W. Norton and Company, 1990)

3–4.   Carbon emissions by country: Ibid., pp. 5–6

9.   Acid rain, dead lakes: Lester Brown et al., *State of the World 1988: A Worldwatch Institute Report* (New York: W. W. Norton and Company, 1988), p. 13

7. Railway construction: E. McNall Burns, R. W. Hull, R. Lerner, and S. Meacham, *World Civilizations*, 7th ed. (New York: W. W. Norton and Company, 1986)

12. Carbon emissions: Brown et al., *State of the World 1990*, pp. 18–20

22–23. Carbon emissions: Brown et al., *State of the World 1990*, p. 18

CHAPTER 4

25. Sigmund Freud, *Civilization and Its Discontents* (New York: W. W. Norton and Company, 1961)

35. Home size: Nick Ravo, "Buyers Insist a Bigger House Is Better," *New York Times*, Nov. 24 '91

CHAPTER 5

47. Java: World Resources Institute Report, 1989

49. NRC, *Alternative Agriculture*, pp. 34–35

48. 1,100 miles per bite: Charis Conn and Henna Silverman, *What Counts: The Complete Harper's Index* (New York: Henry Holt and Company, 1991)

51. $33 billion diet: Molly O'Neill, "Congress Looking into the Diet Business," NYT, Mar. 29 '90

53. Farm size: John Fraser Hart, *The Land That Feeds Us* (New York: W. W. Norton and Company, 1991)

53. "increase health risks . . .": National Research Council, *Alternative Agriculture* (Washington, D.C.: National Academy Press, 1989)

54. Boeing 747 consumption: Boeing 747 Alitalia cockpit crew

55. Food dollar breakdown: NRC, *Alternative Agriculture*, pp. 35–38

56–57. Freud, *Civilization and Its Discontents*

CHAPTER 6

62. Samuel Beckett, *All That Fall* (London: Faber and Faber, Limited, 1957)

68. William H. Kolberg and Foster C. Smith, "New Track For Blue Collar Workers," NYT, Feb. 9 '92

70. Wage Drop: Marc Levinson, "Living on the Edge," *Newsweek*, Nov. 4 '91; and Peter Kilborn, "Middle Class Feels Betrayed," NYT, Jan. 12 '92
70. Length of work: Juliet B. Schor, *The Overworked American* (New York: Basic Books, 1992)
70. Percentage of women working: Levinson, "Living on the Edge," *Newsweek*, Nov. 4 '91
70. Family income: Louis Uchitelle, "Trapped in the Impoverished Middle Class," NYT, Nov. 17 '91
70. Crime statistics: Robert Suro, "Driven by Fear: Crime and Its Amplified Echoes Are Rearranging People's Lives," NYT, Feb. 9 '92
70–71. Layoffs: Steve Lohr, "Executives Expect Many 1991 Layoffs To Be Permanent," NYT, Dec. 16 '91; Daron P. Levin, "General Motors to Cut 70,000 Jobs," NYT, Dec. 18 '91; and "Hudson Valley Reels Under Impact of I.B.M. Cuts," Lisa W. Foderaro, NYT, Dec. 18 '91
71. Banking layoff reaction: Peter T. Kilborn, "Bleak Economy Shattering Job Security in Banking," NYT, Jan. 26 '92
71. Retirement benefits: Barbara Presley Noble, "Endangered Retiree Health Benefits," NYT, Dec. 20 '91
72. Louis Bromfield, *At Malabar* (Baltimore: Johns Hopkins University Press, 1988)
73. *Newsweek* poll, Nov. 4 '91
73–75. Layoffs: B. Drummond Ayres, Jr., "Shadow of Pessimism Eclipses a Dream," NYT, Feb. 9 '92; Steve Lohr, "Accepting Harsh Realities of a Blue-Collar Recession," NYT, Dec. 25 '91; and Louis Uchitelle, "Trapped in the Impoverished Middle Class," NYT, Nov. 17 '91
75. Gillsons: Marc Levinson, "Living on the Edge," *Newsweek*, Nov. 4 '91
75. Julia Carlisle, "Young, Privileged, and Unemployed," NYT, Apr. 4 '91
75. Turnbull, *The Mountain People*
82. Ritchie P. Lowry, *Good Money* (New York: W. W. Norton and Company, 1991)

CHAPTER 8

86. White and Yanos quotes: B. Drummond Ayres, "Shadow of Pessimism Eclipses a Dream," NYT, Feb. 9 '92

87. U.S. Department of Agriculture, 1987; and U.S. Census of Agriculture, 1985

87. NRC, *Alternative Agriculture*, p. 54

87. Rachel Carson, *Silent Spring* (Boston: Houghton Mifflin Company, 1962)

87. Farm population: Hart, *The Land That Feeds Us*; and NRC, *Alternative Agriculture*

87–88. Bromfield, *At Malabar*

89. Hart, *The Land That Feeds Us*

89–90. Changing American farm: Johnson, Dirk, "A Quiet Exodus by Young Leaves the Future of Family Farms in Doubt," NYT, June 9 '92, p. 22

94–95. Eliot Coleman, *The New Organic Grower* (London: Cassell Publishers, Limited, 1989)

95. Pesticides: Lester Brown et al., *State of the World 1988: A Worldwatch Institute Report*, "Controlling Toxic Chemicals," pp. 119–27

95. Pesticides: Helen Caldicott, *If You Love This Planet* (New York: W. W. Norton and Company, 1992)

95. Brown et al., *State of the World 1988*, pp. 119–27

96. Carson, *Silent Spring*

96. Pesticides: Brown et al., *State of the World 1988*, p. 122

97. Cigarettes: unsigned article, NYT, OpEd page, June 28, 1992

98. Interview with Dr. Epstein, Professor, Dept. of Environmental Medicine: quoted in *Village Voice* article on breast cancer in women

98–99. Elaine Dodge and Christy Law, "Poisoned Meat from Canada," NYT, May 31 '91

99–100. Keith Schneider, "E.P.A., in a Reversal, Lifts a Ban on Farm Chemicals," NYT, Feb. 13 '92

101–102. NRC, *Alternative Agriculture*, Executive Summary and pp. 68–69

104–105. Bromfield, *At Malabar*

118. Felicity Barringer, "Census Reflects Restless Nation," NYT, Dec. 20 '91; and Barringer, "Those Lights in Big Cities Get Brighter," NYT, Dec. 17 '91

119.   Freud, *Civilization and Its Discontents*
119.   Quote of F. C. Hall: "Report from the Field of an Endless War," NYT, March 12 '89
120.   Cancer: Karen Wright, "Living by the Numbers," NYT Magazine, Dec. 15 '91
122.   Ralph Burns et al., *World Civilizations*
124.   List of vital human needs in cities: Mumford, *The Urban Prospect*
125.   U.S. Census Bureau; and NYT, Felicity Barringer, "Census Reflects Restless Nature," Dec. 20 '91
125.   Violent youths: NYT; *La Republica*, Italy; and RAI Uno (Italian television interview)
128.   Potential taxes on rich: Victor Perlo, "Who the Rich Are and What They Should Pay," NYT, Dec. 1 '91; and John Cushman, Jr., "Federal Government Expenditures by Department," NYT, Jan., '91

CHAPTER 11

131.   Wilton quote: Molly O'Neill, NYT, Aug. 23 '92
136.   House advertisement: NYT, July '92

CHAPTER 12

149.   Barbie dolls: Harper's Index, *Harper's Magazine*, Nov. '91
151.   Carnegie Foundation report: Susan Chira, "Report Says Too Many Aren't Ready for School," NYT, Dec. 8 '91

CHAPTER 13

151.   C.E.O.'s salary: Conn and Silverman, *What Counts: The Complete Harper's Index*
152–153.   Jane Gross, "Afraid and Hurt, Young Turn to Clinics," NYT, Jan. 28 '92
154.   National Geographic survey: Caldicott, *If You Love This Planet*
155.   Department of Education report: Karen De Witt, "U.S. Schooling: 20 Years of Mediocrity," NYT, Aug. 14 '91
155.   Carnegie report: Susan Chira, NYT, Dec. 8 '91
155.   Lewis Mumford, *The Urban Prospect*

158. William Clayton, "For Students, Steinbeck and Orwell Can't Match Cliffs Notes," NYT, June 14, 1992

162. 70,000 chemicals: Brown et al., *State of the World 1988*

CHAPTER 14

169. Clifford T. Morgan and Richard A. King, *Introduction to Psychology* (New York: McGraw-Hill Publishers, 1966)

171. American Association of University Women survey: Maureen Dowd, NYT, Feb. 6 '92

175. Morgan and King, *Introduction to Psychology*

CHAPTER 15

183. Roper Study: Conn and Silverman, *What Counts: The Complete Harper's Index*

190. Soundbites: Kiku Adatto, "T.V. Tidbits Starve Democracy," NYT, Dec. 10 '89

190. Karen DeWitt, "U.S. Schooling: 20 Years of Mediocrity," NYT, Aug. 14 '91

190. Magazines: Conn and Silverman, *What Counts: The Complete Harper's Index*

CHAPTER 16

194. Anthony Lewis, "Dollars and Cynicism," NYT, June 28 '92

195. 1988 Presidential elections: Everett C. Ladd, Jr., *The American Polity*, 4th edition (New York: W. W. Norton and Company, 1991), pp. 366 and 401

196. Lawrence Wright, NYT

196. Theodore Lowi & Benjamin Ginsberg, *American Government*, Second Edition (New York: W. W. Norton and Company, 1992)

197. Sylvia Nasar, "The Rich Get Richer, but Never the Same Way Twice," NYT Aug. 16 '92

198. Caldicott, *If You Love This Planet*, pp. 181–182

199. Lewis, "Dollars and Cynicism," NYT, June 28 '92

204–205. Caldicott, *If You Love This Planet*

CHAPTER 17

215. Coleman, *The New Organic Grower*
217. Beverly Smith, "More a Way of Life," *The Globe and Mail*, Dec. 28 '91
227. Wolf Von Eckhardt, *A Place to Live: The Crisis of the Cities* (New York: Delacorte Press, 1968)